Upward, Outward, Inward

Upward
Outward
Inward

Mitsuo Fukuda

**Translated by
Simon Cozens**

*W*ide Margin

Originally published in Japan
under the title KEITEN-AIJIN by
Jibikiami Publishing, Tokyo.

Published in 2010 by Wide Margin,
90 Sandyleaze, Gloucester, GL2 0PX, UK
http://www.wide-margin.co.uk/

ISBN 978-0-9565943-1-0

Scripture quotations are taken from the New English
Translation except where otherwise noted.
http://net.bible.org/

Printed and bound in Great Britain by
Lightning Source, Milton Keynes

For Fumiko with all my love.

In Memoriam

Yasukiyo Fukuda 1924-2007
Kinuyo Fukuda 1931-2007
Hatsue Saijo 1924-2009
Henry Carlton Kenney   1935-2002

Contents

F Foreword

In the early days of the Reformation in Scotland, the Lord raised up a man, John Knox, whose passion for his country and for the work of the Lord led him to say, "Give me Scotland or I die." In Mitsuo, God has raised up such a man for Japan. And just as the Reformation was going to change the structure and the theology of the existing church in Scotland, so Mitsuo's work will change the structure and the theology of the currently prevailing church models in Japan and, potentially, elsewhere. This is not so much a statement of Mitsuo's drive and personality as it is a recognition that God is doing similar things around the world in this generation.

Stories abound of the dramatic and transformation impact of simple church movements around the world. In the summer of 2010 I have read about a house church movement in India that has baptized over one million people in the past year. During this same summer I have read via the Associated Press in papers around the world of the impact of house church movements in the West. It does not seem to matter if you are dealing with the affluence and sophistication of Osaka, Tokyo or New York, or the poverty and neglect of a developing world slum city. The people have the same right to know of the love of God and the meaning that can and will be brought into their lives as they come to know that love. Mitsuo's down-to-earth and practical book will help anyone understand how to do this.

But God's love is not an intangible. It is demonstrated through relationships—with Jesus and with other people—and this is the power of what Mitsuo writes. Drawing from his experience working with groups of all types, Mitsuo gives us a picture of what church can be like. As the title leads us to understand, "Upward, Outward, Inward" implies more than just the direction of the relationships that we form; rather, it stresses the importance of the order in which these relationships develop. If you do not have the connection with the Lord, then there is really nothing to give. But similarly, if your core DNA does not have what is necessary to direct your attention outwards, then however "deep" your inner walk with God, something is going to be missing. It is this focus on mission, very practically expressed, that runs through the heart of this book's message.

From the start to the finish, this book stresses that we must live what we are learning.

Join Mitsuo on his journey into a life of dependency on God.

DR. TONY DALE
Co-author with Felicity Dale and George Barna of
The Rabbit and the Elephant
Co-founder and President of House 2 House ministries.
Chairman and Founder of The Karis Group.

T Thanks

This book is the result of a collaboration with my friends; we spent many journeys together, trained a great variety of people together, cried a lot together, laughed a lot together, shared happy times together, shared struggles together, and discovered the will of God together. Each one of those friends on the journey is my pride and joy, my family. Without their support, this book could not have been written.

Thanks to Tony Dale, for his kind words and for taking the time to write the foreword; to Wolfgang Simson, David Garrison, John White, Neil Cole and many others for their words of encouragement. Simon Cozens used his excellent linguistic ability and spiritual insight to turn this into natural English.

Waichiro Taniguchi at Jibikiami Press gave me a lot of practical advice. Thank you.

I **Introduction**

In the summer of 2004, I visited Phuket, in Thailand. I woke up early in the morning and wandered along the deserted coastline. The sandy beaches stretched for miles, and the waves from the clear Andaman sea broke silently on the shore. Tiny grains of sand scritched below my feet.

I stood still, and scooped up a handful of sand. Watching the grains of sand fall from my fingers, I found that I was talking to myself. "There's so many; too many to count. The whole bottom of the ocean is filled with so many grains of sand."

Just as I said that, I heard the words of God: "So shall your descendants be."

I fell to my knees in that place and began to weep. I was overwhelmed by God's great love for the people of my country and by His great generosity, that he would entrust such a responsibility to a sinner like me. God had made a promise to Abraham in Genesis 22:17: "I will indeed bless you, and I will greatly multiply your descendants so that they will be as countless as the stars in the sky or the grains of sand on the seashore. Your descendants will take possession of the strongholds of their enemies." It seemed like God wanted to bind himself to that kind of contract with this generation as well.

In Japan, it's been 460 years since the start of Catholic mission and 150 years since the start of Protestant mission. In that time, much time and many resources have been generously poured into mission work in that country. But Japan, like a barren woman, has not been able to bring about generation upon generation of Christians. God wants to say this to such a country: "Shout for joy, O barren one who has not given birth! Give a joyful shout and cry out, you who have not been in labor!" (Isaiah 54:1) The time of harvest is drawing near.

So if we are on the eve of that harvest, what should we be thinking about? If the promise to Abraham would come to pass here in about ten years time, then maybe we should keep praying until then. But if we're looking for the realization of that promise *now*, the time has come to take a step of faith *today*.

Just like the wise virgins in Matthew 25:1-13 took the practical step of preparing oil, we should be continuing to pray, but we should also taking practical steps towards action: we should be raising up workers for the harvest. What would happen if God were to bring ten new believers into the church in a single day? Would we be able to disciple them? What if it were a hundred people in a week? Do you think it's possible to receive a thousand new believers a month? If a million people were saved, would the church be ready to disciple them?[1]

The Lord wants us to prepare workers for the harvest.

What sort of people do these workers need to be? First, they need to be people who listen to what God is saying. In 1 John 2:27, John writes

> "Now as for you, the anointing that you received from him resides in you, and you have no need for anyone to teach you."

1   Tony and Felicity and the H2H team, "Are You A Missionary or An Imposter?" *House2house E-Letter*, December 7, 2009. http://e-letter.house2house.com/2009/12/07/are-you-a-missionary-or-an-imposter/ (accessed April 09, 2010)

The people of God with the Spirit of God have the ability to hear the voice of God. This is not just something for special people; "ordinary men" (Acts 4:13) can listen to the voice of God and carry out His harvest mission. The most ordinary Christian can, every moment of every day, fix their eyes on Jesus and receive a message from the Lord. (Acts 2:17-18)

The purpose of our getting a message like this is not, fundamentally, for our own satisfaction. God uses us to pass on His message to others. We're basically God's postal workers.

The second requirement for harvest workers is that they need to be sent out by God to serve other people. We follow Jesus, who came "not to be served but to serve," (Matthew 20:28) and just like him, we are sent out to become servants of others.

I mentioned postal workers, and like postal workers, we don't just *receive* the message; we pass it on. When God is telling us "this morning, call so-and-so and encourage her" or "listen really carefully to what's being said around the table at lunchtime" or "bake a cake and take it with you," then He's leading us into an action that's based on love. Our very existence becomes "a letter of Christ." (2 Corinthians 3:3)

But even if one fantastic person decides that they're going to become a faithful postal worker, they're not going to be able to deal with the whole harvest on their own. Jesus says that "the harvest is plentiful, but the workers are few." (Luke 10:2) What we need to be doing is building up more and more workers. We can't just hold on to the baton of discipleship that we've received, but we need to be able to pass it on to others. The third requirement for a harvest worker is that they need to die to self and pass on the baton of what they have received to other people.

Upward, Outward, Inward

Discipling others is dying to self. Jesus said that "unless a kernel of wheat falls into the ground and dies, it remains by itself alone. But if it dies, it produces much grain." (John 12:24) You won't see too many generations while you stay alive. "If anyone wants to become my follower, he must deny himself, take up his cross daily, and follow me." (Luke 9:23; see also 1 Corinthians 15:31) People who follow that commandment will be examples of "taking up their cross" to those they disciple.

You don't need to bring in a specialist for this kind of discipleship. It's something that can be done by anyone who can accept what is on God's heart. It's not something that can be learnt from lectures in the classroom, but it requires you to pass on simple skills through actual practice. First, the discipler gives the example, and the disciples observe; then the disciples help out the discipler for a time. As the disciples mature, they begin to take on more and more of the responsibility as they help out until they can do things without the discipler. In this way, skills can be effectively passed on from one person to another. Passing on the baton isn't a matter of going to particular events or being part of particular organizations, but is something that can be done anywhere, any time, by anyone who is prepared to follow God.

By God's grace, and through eight years of working all this out by trial and error on the mission field, I've managed to put together a plan and an implementation strategy for a grass-roots discipleship training scheme. This is a summary of what I've learnt through that process.

What's special about this training programme is that it's simple and it's catalytic. I've tried to make it as simple as possible so that as many people as possible can get hold of it; if the baton is going to pass from one person to another, it's vitally important that the baton is 'light.' But we need to be careful that it isn't so simple that the essentials are left behind. So at the same time as being simple, we have to aim for it to be catalytic. What I mean by catalytic is that it promotes direct communication between those who attend the training and God Himself, and it provides a channel for the transformation and growth that's going on inside people.

So, for instance, the devotions are made up of simple questions for God, and then center around listening to God's voice answering those questions. By inviting people into a place where they can talk directly to God for themselves, we do not need to concern ourselves with details like how exactly to pray but we can allow people can discover God's heart through fellowship with Him.

I'm convinced that if this sort of baton-passing takes place in the lives of ordinary Christians, they can raise up harvest workers, and then raise up disciplers of harvest workers, and then raise up disciplers of disciplers, and on and on.

So then. Let's begin.

Honor God, Love Neighbour

1

For an audience of one

Once upon a time, there was a very talented young pianist; he was still an innocent child. When the performance finished, everyone in the audience rose up in a standing ovation until the calls for encore filled the concert hall.

But the young man, standing in the wings, did not respond to the cries from the audience. The conductor turned and said to him, "Everyone is on their feet calling for an encore!" But the pianist replied, "That old man in the middle of the second floor balcony isn't standing up."

The conductor replied wearily. "Maybe his hearing isn't very good, or his legs are weak and he can't stand up easily. Everyone else is standing up." But the pianist said sorrowfully, "No, that man is my piano teacher."

The applause of the audience didn't mean very much to the young piano player. Even though there were many people in the hall, he was playing for an audience of one. Even if nobody else in the audience appreciated his playing, if his beloved piano teacher, who knew him best of all, had liked it, then he would gladly have given an encore.

Upward, Outward, Inward

In Acts 7, we see Stephen giving a speech before a whole crowd of people. Unlike the pianist in our example, the crowd was very angry with Stephen—we're told that "when they heard these things, they became furious and ground their teeth at him." (Acts 7:54) At that time, only one person appreciated his speech.

> "But Stephen, full of the Holy Spirit, looked intently toward heaven and saw the glory of God, and Jesus standing at the right hand of God. 'Look!' he said. 'I see the heavens opened, and the Son of Man standing at the right hand of God!'" (Acts 7:55-56)

Being rejected or ignored by people is hard; but I think that if I can see Jesus, sitting at the right hand of God, sticking up for me, I would be satisfied. One of my favorite verses is Psalm 27:10: "Even if my father and mother abandoned me, the Lord would take me in." How much of an encouragement must it have been for Stephen to see the glory of the Lord![1]

If at the end of my life, I can hear Him say, "You did well. I was always watching you. You did a good job. I know that you gave it your all," then all the strife and suffering will have been worth it. I spend every day of my life looking forward to that; I think, if that's going to be my reward, then I today I'm going to live my life with all that I've got.

God Himself will make us perfect

I don't think there could be a better ending to our life's story than to see Jesus standing up for us in those final moments. There is no hiding place in dying, and the way we die is a kind of microcosm of the way we've lived. A

1   Leith Anderson. *Leadership That Works: Hope and Direction for Church and Parachurch Leaders in Today's Complex World.* Minneapolis, MN: Bethany House, 2001. pp.210-211.

Honor God, Love Neighbour

life lived faithfully day by day before God is the premise which sets up a beautiful final scene.

But there's also an sense in which God Himself has the responsibility for closing the book of our life. (See Deuteronomy 32:10-12) Even if we are walking faithfully before God, that is only by His grace and not something that we should boast about. (Luke 17:10) God is the one who is teaching me and enabling me to offer up myself to Him as I stay in fellowship with Him.

My life is "God's workmanship" (Ephesians 2:10); it is God who started it, and He will bring it to perfection. Paul himself, writing to churches in Philippi which were facing a mountain of problems, wrote that, "I am sure of this very thing, that the one who began a good work in you will perfect it until the day of Christ Jesus." (Philippians 1:6)

An aunt of mine, who's died now, used to do a lot of embroidery, and made all kinds of beautiful lacework tapestries. If you turn over a tapestry, it's very hard to distinguish the pattern, and all you can see are knots and hanging threads. But when you see the finished piece, you work it out: "I see, that black thread there was used to show off this part of the pattern here..." When our life's mission is fulfilled, God turns our life over and sees the completed pattern, and He declares it to be beautiful.[2]

Over the course of our lives, we will inevitably meet with difficult circumstances, and there are times when we'll want to cry out "why did that happen to me?" That's because we can't see the other side of the tapestry. But when, like Stephen, we look up into heaven, (Acts 7:55) we will meet the gaze of Jesus who sees the whole tapestry of our lives. God himself completes his workmanship in us by weaving trials and hardship into our lives.

If you're maturing fine wines, the right climate is indispensable; in the same way, the trials and tribulations

3

2   Corrie Ten Boom, *Tramp for the Lord*, p. 12

of our lives are not mere accidents: they are indispensable to making God's workmanship in us complete. Even Jesus "learned obedience through the things he suffered, and was perfected in this way." (Hebrews 5:8-9) So everything that we go through in life has a meaning.

If our lives are God's workmanship, then how can we say things like, "I'm such a rubbish person"? If we speak ill of an artwork, then indirectly we're running down the person who made it. A Picasso picture is priceless, even if it's unfinished or just a sketch, and in the same way, our lives might be incomplete and unrefined, but because of the greatness of God, our lives are valuable because they're His work.

In a sense, a piece of artwork is a reflection of its creator. All of Creation reflects in part the beauty of the Creator. But the Bible tells us that humans alone are "made in the image of God." (Genesis 1:27) This is the unique majesty of humanity: we are God's expression, God's poetry.

Wouldn't it be amazing if everyone recognized the fact that they are God's workmanship, and they could start each day excited about what God is going to create in them that day?

It actually takes practice to rejoice and receive the fact that we're God's workmanship. This is because most people grow up hearing words and messages that harm their own self-respect. Even now, we're surrounded by messages that tell us that we're no good. So we need to listen every day to the voice of God who made us, and every day we need to take hold of these words of hope: "My life is valuable because it is the masterpiece of a master artist, and He will bring it to completion."

Honour God, Love Neighbor

How should we respond to this amazing mercy that God pours into our lives? There are two ways for us to show our love for God.

The first is to show our joy. If you've put a lot of time and energy into getting someone a present, and the person you give it to doesn't show any emotion at all, it feels really discouraging and unsatisfying. I think when God sees the smiling faces of people as they receive the gifts that He's given them, He considers it a reward for the sacrifice that He made.

Our Father in heaven gives us good gifts! (Matthew 7:11) Paul expresses the generosity of God like this:

> Indeed, he who did not spare his own Son, but gave him up for us all—how will he not also, along with him, freely give us all things?

If God has given us everything, up to and including his Son, shouldn't I then at least give Him a smile? So the first way to show our love for God—and to live out the Gospel—is by always being thankful before Him, and always rejoicing before Him. Wouldn't it be a really good way to love Him by "continually offering up a sacrifice of praise to God, that is, the fruit of our lips, acknowledging His name"?

John puts in this way in 1 John 5:3: "For this is the love of God: that we keep His commandments." If we sing "I love you, I love you," but we don't keep His commandments at all, then we're not really loving Him. So another way to show our love for God is to do what He asks of us. "Certainly, obedience is better than sacrifice." (1 Samuel 15:22) God is a master of communication: as we ask every day "How much do you love me?", He expresses His love for us; and as we ask every day "How should I live?", He shows us the way He wants us to go.

Upward, Outward, Inward

If you have a satellite navigation system in your car, you can arrive at your destination even if you don't know the area. In just the same way, God is watching us from heaven and is able to guide us as to the route that we ought to take in our lives. The safest and the fullest way to live our lives is the way that God teaches us. Honoring God, then, is doing what He asks of us. If we obey, then we can give the work over to God, as He works to complete our lives.

What is it that God is asking us to do? Jesus puts it plainly: "Love your neighbor as yourself." (Luke 10:27) To give us eternal life, Jesus made himself nothing, took on the nature of a servant and finally gave his life up for us. (See Philippians 2:5–11) God tells us that we should serve others in the same way. The reason that we listen to God's voice is not fundamentally for our own benefit, but for God's and for our neighbors' benefit. God's masterpieces are filled with the spirit of serving their neighbors.

I sum up this whole idea—honoring God and obeying His command to love our neighbors—in four words: Honor God, Love Neighbor. On top of that, the central core of discipleship is dying to self and raising up people who will raise up other disciples.

'Upward, Outward, Inward' teaches us how to practically work out Jesus's teaching of 'Honor God, Love Neighbor' in a way that's appropriate to our daily lives. The aim is that within forty-eight hours of making a decision for Christ, someone will be able to lead others to Him and be able to teach *them* the fundamentals of Honor God, Love Neighbor discipleship.

The 'Upward' in 'Upward, Outward, Inward' means relationship with God, 'Outward' means relationship with the world, and 'Inward' means relationship with ourselves and with our friends. It's a simple pattern that anyone can remember and anyone can pass on to another person. In the next chapter, we'll explain this in more detail.

2 Snatches of God's Teaching

Musical parody

I want to introduce you to a parody song. Sing it to the tune of "With A Little Help From My Friends."

I will rejoice that my name is in heav'n,
I will listen to the voice of God.
I will follow anywhere that my Lord goes,
Carrying the cross of Christ.

Oh, I will serve those He puts around me,
Oh, I will talk about the Kingdom of God,
Oh, I will see people come to Him.

There are some simple actions to go along with this song, and people who came to the first of my training sessions memorize both the song and the actions. Even a two-year old baby who couldn't speak picked up the actions, without anyone teaching her, and started to dance along. It's so simple that anyone can remember it. I've heard that some women have really taken to this song and have made a habit of singing it when they get it up first thing in the morning.

Upward, Outward, Inward

This song sums up the essence of our Upward, Outward, Inward teaching. If you can remember these short verses, you can get hold of the whole of the training and review it just by singing along. One aim of this kind of training is to give you some simple words and images to repeat and remember.

When doing the training in other countries, I choose songs that people there know well and sing them as parodies. Last year we went to one country and found a well-known folk song that everyone in that area knew, and got them all singing along with it. One of the attendees, going back to his home town after the training finished, woke up at three in the morning and started singing the song. His neighbors heard it and started asking him questions, so he explained the meaning to them and people began to believe in Jesus.In the end, about 50 people were saved within three and a half months.

Simple and short

The most important commandment in the whole Bible is Deuteronomy 6:5: "You must love the LORD your God with your whole mind, your whole being, and all your strength." The following verses then explain how to put that into practice:

> These words I am commanding you today must be kept in mind, and you must teach them to your children and speak of them as you sit in your house, as you walk along the road, as you lie down, and as you get up. You should tie them as a reminder on your forearm and fasten them as symbols on your forehead. Inscribe them on the doorframes of your houses and gates.

Tying words to your arms or writing them on your doorframes gives you a way to repeat and remember them. It's simple and it's easy to understand.

If you've been given good advice, put it into practice—that's just common sense. God's chosen way for you to live will take root in you and become your natural behavior as you continually put it into practice through repeating and remembering. You need to work to repeat and remember these new insights so that what you remember becomes established in your actions.[1]

James explains this point very well:

> For if someone merely listens to the message and does not live it out, he is like someone who gazes at his own face in a mirror. For he gazes at himself and then goes out and immediately forgets what sort of person he was. But the one who peers into the perfect law of liberty and fixes his attention there, and does not become a forgetful listener but one who lives it out—he will be blessed in what he does.

Even if you're someone who takes a long time to put on make-up before you go out, you don't really pay much attention to what your face is like as you go about your daily life, unless you're particularly self-conscious. In the same way, people can't apply the Bible to their daily lives unless they make an effort to really get into the word of God in the "ordinary places" of their lives—not just in the special quiet times, the spiritual equivalent of sitting in front of a mirror. If they don't put it into practice, then no matter how carefully you might teach them, they will walk away and forget about what they've heard.

This is how the Psalmist describes someone who puts the Lord's teaching into practice: "He finds pleasure in obeying the Lord's commands; he meditates on his commands day and night." If you're going to meditate on God's commands day and night, they need to be in a package that's simple and easy to get to know.

9

1   David Rock, *Quiet Leadership: Six Steps to Transforming Performance at Work.* New York, NY: Collins, 2006.

Since they're simple, they can easily be taught to somebody else. In fact, don't even think of it as teaching—think of it as being like them picking up a song. Even children can pick up the important bits very quickly. However, if you're not careful to keep the contents of what you're teaching simple, you end up with this huge system of teachings that requires a special person to learn and pass on.

> "This commandment I am giving you today is not too difficult for you, nor is it too remote. It is not in heaven, as though one must say, "Who will go up to heaven to get it for us and proclaim it to us so we may obey it?" And it is not across the sea, as though one must say, "Who will cross over to the other side of the sea and get it for us and proclaim it to us so we may obey it?" For the thing is very near you–it is in your mouth and in your mind so that you can do it." (Deuteronomy 30:11–14)

Jesus' teaching was not difficult. It's not something that can only be done by a "master" after a long period of training. Anyone can learn from the Bible. Anyone can keep its words in mind and appreciate them. Anyone can follow God as they go about their daily lives. Anyone can raise up disciples.

KISS–Keep It Simple and Short–is the watchword of this movement.

Fractal Structures

It's also important, and very effective, for such a package of teachings to be "fractal." A fractal is an image which, when you look at any part of it close up, you see the structure of the whole. Wherever you zoom in, you find similarities with the original, just as if it had little copies of itself in minature inside it.[2]

2   Neil Cole, *Organic Church: Growing Faith Where Life Happens*. San Francisco, CA: Jossey-Bass, 2005. pp.128-129.

So for instance, in our training, the song that we introduced at the start of this chapter is an expression of its simple theology, but everything that we teach after the song—the devotions, the accountability groups, right up to the leadership development training—they all have the same basic structure. This is because it gives you a comprehensive understanding of what it means to follow Jesus—so that no matter what the circumstances, you can remember the same pattern.

To give an example of this fractal structure, in Upward Outward Inward training, we often use the technique of asking questions to God or to one another. The questions are divided into three areas, and we'll deal with them in the relevant chapters, but they are precisely designed to keep your attention focused.

For example, in morning devotions, you'll ask God the question, "How should I share the Gospel today and what words should I use?" In weekly small groups, people will ask each other the same question: "Who have you shared the Gospel with in this past week?" When coaching leaders, we use the same sorts of question again: "What does the church need to deal with to help families of non-Christians to get saved?" and "How can you help the people that you are leading to joyfully share the gospel with others?" So we've made a framework whereby this sort of question is repeated over and over, in daily devotions, in weekly accountability groups and in monthly coaching sessions, and so it stays at the top of your mind.

A well put-together presentation or a powerful workshop might motivate an audience for a time; but just like someone who walks away from a mirror and then forgets his own face, people often end up quickly forgetting the content. A preacher or a seminar presenter must really beat themselves up when they find out that, no matter how much emphasis they've put on their content, people's lives don't change. What determines whether or not you can keep on putting the word of God into practice is whether or not you have a "framework" to really focus you onto the important things in life.

So we've laid out the benefits of having a simple but a fractal pattern to help put God's will into practice, but here's another question: Is that alone going to bring about a new move of God?

The answer is no. The one thing I want to make sure you understand is that the structure is not the thing that gives life. It's actually life that gives birth to the structure. "I planted, Apollos watered, but God caused it to grow." (1 Co. 3:6) If you make a vine trellis with the perfect structure for the type of grape and the climate, that should help you get a good harvest of grapes; but even if the trellis helps the vine to grow, the trellis cannot bring a new vine into being. The trellis is not alive; the vine is alive. Life gives birth to life.

When God sent the wind of his Spirit, the Church advanced like a boat catching the wind. Upward Outward Inward training was developed little by little, through trial and error, like a boat putting up a sail to catch the wind of what God was teaching us. Even now we're still changing the format of it as we see how it works in practice. What I want to do is to go sailing, as it were, with people who really would like to be involved in catching the wind of the Spirit and seeing the discipling of the whole world.

When you focus on simple, short, snatches of God's teaching, you'll be able to put His will into practice.

3 Up-Out-In, not Up-In-Out

Inward before Outward?

When you're on a plane, they'll tell you that in the event of a loss of cabin pressure, oxygen masks will automatically drop from the ceiling. Then they'll tell you that you need to put on your own mask before helping any children around you to put on their masks. This is because in cases of sudden decompression, you lose consciousness within 20 seconds, and if you lose consciousness, you won't be in any position to help those around you.

About ten years ago, I used this example to teach that Christian workers had to support themselves first: results-driven, perfectionist workaholics (like myself) need to make sure that they regularly get away from the mission field and take time out with God, with their family and friends, and with nature, to rest their minds and their bodies. Jesus himself said "Let the one who believes in me drink. Just as the scripture says, 'From within him will flow rivers of living water.'" (John 7:38) In other words, if you're blessed yourself, then you can let that blessing flow out of you; but you can't quench another person's thirst if you are thirsty yourself.

Upward, Outward, Inward

And so I thought "Before Outward, we should have Inward," and so the first drafts of Upward Outward Inward used to be called, of course, Upward Inward Outward. But now I've realised that the Outward needs to come first, and so it's called Upward Outward Inward.

The reason for this is that when someone first comes to Christ, if you tell them that first they need to get healed, get cleaned up, get mature, and get filled with the Spirit before they do anything, you end up shutting them away and making them inwards-focused. Getting healed and cleaned and mature is not something that happens overnight and then it's done. It's a process of spiritual formation that takes place throughout your whole life, like the way that a tree bears fruit throughout its whole life; if you wait until that process is completed before you do anything, you'll miss the opportunity to be going outwards. On top of that, "being filled with the Spirit" is a very subjective thing, and there's a chance that you'll end up endlessly worried about whether or not you're filled up *enough*!

Believe and begin speaking

In John 4:3–42, the Samaritan woman had a short conversation with Jesus and then immediately went out to talk to people in her village. She did not talk about the cross or the resurrection; the message that she had to tell to others was "that man told me everything that I did." Jesus put that Gentile woman to work in saving the town, even though he'd only met her that same day.

The madman of Gesara was also sent back into his home town immediately after he was freed from his legion of demons. (Luke 8:28–39) Jesus didn't say "follow me about, get some study, learn the right doctrines, polish your evangelistic skills, and then you can put together a crack church planting team, and *then* take them into your home town." Instead, Jesus told this man, who actually wanted to become one of his followers, to "return to your home, and declare what God has done for you." This man, rough and ready and only just saved, could make a contribution to the kingdom of God just as he was.

This is because, from the instant that someone believes in Jesus, there's an "extraordinary power" (2 Co. 4:7) that is placed in their "jar of clay". For example, when you've felt weak, you've probably had someone encourage you with 2 Timothy 1:7: "For God did not give us a Spirit of fear but of power and love and self-control." In a time like that, it doesn't make sense to pray, "Oh God, I'm feeling fearful, so please give me a spirit of power and love and self-control"—because you've already been given one!

When I got married to my wife, I only had a couple of dollars in my pocket. In the cheap flat that we rented, there was hardly anything that belonged to me; she brought all the furniture with her into the marriage. But from the day that we got married, those weren't *her* things any more—they belonged to us as a couple.

The same thing happened when I believed in Jesus. In the instant of conversion, I was made a "co-heir with Christ." (Romans 8:17; see also Galatians 4:1) I was connected to Christ just like a "husband and wife" (Ephesians 5:32) or a "vine and its branches" (John 15:5) or a "head and its body." (Colossians 1:18) From the time that I believed in Jesus and the Spirit came to live in me, everything belonged to me, whether "the world or life or death or the present or the future." (1 Corinthians 3:22) And did I do anything special, right at the start of my Christian life, to earn all this amazing stuff? No! It's all by grace, all bought by the atonement of Jesus on the cross.

And *when* did I get into this situation? When did streams of living water become to spring from the depths of my heart? Was it after I became mature and was made clean? No, this is the spiritual state of everyone, right down to the youngest spiritual baby. Faith is a matter of knowing and believing this reality.

Every single person who believes in Christ has "clothed themselves with Christ." (Gal 3:27) It's actually as we go out "externally" to "make disciples of all nations" (Matthew 28:19) that we experience hardships, which in turn produce that "internal" change in us as we come to resemble the likeness of Christ.

The structure of our training

So then, let's explain the basic structure of our training, in order: Upward, Outward, Inward. First, we say that a person lives in three relationships of love: their relationship with God, their relationship with the outside world, and their relationship with themselves or their fellow Christians. This is what we call Upward, Outward and Inward relationships.

If you look at the Chinese character for 'man', or at our stick figure man at the bottom of the page, you'll see that we've written 'upwards', 'outwards' and 'inwards' at the three points on the figure. When we're explaining the

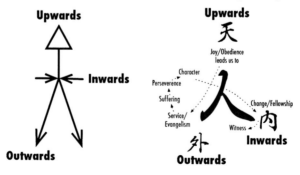

relationships to someone and we draw the figure for them, we start at the top in the 'upward' position. Out of these three types of relationship, the most important is our relationship with God.

We show our love for God in two ways. First, by rejoicing in His unchanging love. God has given us the best possible gift in His Son Jesus, so it's an expression of our love to show our joy and thankfulness to Him every day. It says in Phillipians 3:20 that our citizenship is in heaven. If you have a passport, you might commit a terrible crime but you don't get your passport taken away. God is saying to us that no matter what the circumstances of our lives may be, no matter what we do, we belong to Him. So we can rejoice at any time that "our names are written in heaven" (Luke 10:20)—in other words, in the unchanging love of God.

The second way to show our love is by obeying Him. Jesus said "If anyone loves me, he will obey my word." (John 14:23) Jesus is the good shepherd, and is speaking to his sheep every day. If we listen to his voice and obey it, then we are loving God. As we rejoice in God and obey God, we will come to know the will of God.

And what is the will of God? The will of God is for "all people to be saved and to come to a knowledge of the truth." (1 Timothy 2:4) God wants to enfold everyone in His bosom; that's why we as His disciples introduce those who are "bewildered and helpless, like sheep without a shepherd" to the Good Shepherd. That's why we serve those we meet and why we testify boldly to the Gospel. Our "upward" relationship with God leads naturally to our "outward" relationship with others.

As we go out into the world, sharing that heart of God who "so loved the world that he gave his one and only Son," (John 3:16) we will be faced with "weaknesses, with insults, with troubles, with persecutions and difficulties."

Upward, Outward, Inward

(2 Co. 12:10) But as we continue to live a live of rejoicing in God's love and obedience to His word, our "suffering produces endurance, and endurance, character, and character, hope." (Romans 5:3–4) So although our "outwards" relationship will produce troubles, through the hope that those troubles lead to, we will experience a deep fellowship with God, sharing in the sufferings of Christ, and this will in turn produce the meekness and humility of Christ in our "inward" selves.

As I am changed through this process, so my relationship with others changes too. As my character is transformed in a more and more godly way, it causes me to develop a deeper love for my brothers and sisters in Christ. Showing love in my "inward" relationships means both being fulfilled with the change that is happening in my life, and also showing love for the community of faith that accompanies me.

This love becomes a witness to others: "Everyone will know by this that you are my disciples—if you have love for one another." (John 13:35) The change inside us gives us a missional impulse to go from "inward" to "outward" again.

The three directions of our training are knowing the heart of God, ("upward") going out and introducing people to the good shepherd ("outward") and being transformed through suffering into the likeness of Christ. ("inward")

4 Practicing Being Joyful

Rejoice in the Lord

> "Finally, my brothers and sisters, rejoice in the Lord! To write this again is no trouble to me, and it is a safeguard for you." (Philippians 3:1)

This is a verse from Paul's letter to the churches in Philippi, a letter that came out of prison. The churches beyond those prison walls were facing a whole host of problems. They say that when the cat's away, the mice will play, and Paul's enemies had begun to wield their influence in the churches. We don't know the details, but it's obviously a situation where Paul feels the need to write that "others are busy with their own concerns, not those of Jesus Christ." (Philippians 2:21) On top of that, the church was being attacked by false teachers coming in from outside, and from opposition amongst the leading women inside the church. To top it all off, one of Paul's co-workers was sick and dying.

In the midst of all this mountain of woes, Paul commands them again and again to "rejoice in the Lord!", and encourages them to "do everything without grumbling or arguing" (2:14), to maintain purity of heart when being criticised, to shine as lights of the world. The letter only has four chapters, but the word "rejoice" appears 16 times.

What does it mean to "rejoice in the Lord?" It means to delight in the deep, close relationship that the Lord has brought us into, and to delight in the Lord Himself who invited us into that relationship. The union between God and His people is expressed in a whole range of metaphors. One of them appears in Isaiah 62:5: "As a bridegroom rejoices over a bride, so your God will rejoice over you." Can you imagine how a bridegroom feels as he sees his "bride adorned for her husband" (Rev. 21:2) walking one step at a time down the aisle to meet him? Do you imagine Jesus saying something like "to be honest, I'm not really all that bothered, but it looks like you've made a bit of an effort, so it's all good"? Of course not! God rejoices in our very existence, just like a bridegroom rejoices over a bride.

You can find expressions of the depth of God's love, His emotion and His heart cry all the way through the Bible. For example, there's Jeremiah 31:20: "I still remember them with fondness. So I am deeply moved with pity for them and will surely have compassion on them." There's also Isaiah 49:15: "Can a woman forget her baby who nurses at her breast? Can she withhold compassion from the child she has borne? Even if mothers were to forget, I could never forget you!" Can you imagine the smiling face of an expectant mother as she rubs her tummy, happily exclaiming, "the baby's kicking!" But God says that even if a mother could forget her baby, He cannot forget you! God is always thinking about His people, "even when they sleep." (Psalm 127:2) The sum total of God's thoughts towards me can be found in Psalm 139, verse 18: "If I tried to count them, they would outnumber the grains of sand."

Our union with God is an eternal union. The Bible expresses this by saying that "our citizenship is in heaven." (Philipians 3:20) We can guess that the mission of the disciples, when they went out two-by-two into the towns and villages of Israel, was a great success because they came back to Jesus with joy. (see Luke 10:17) But Jesus points their joy in a different direction: "Nevertheless, do not rejoice that the spirits submit to you, but rejoice that your names stand written in heaven." (Luke 10:20) What does it mean that our names stand written in heaven, that we are recorded in "the book of life"? (Revelation 20:15) It is God's declaration to us that, "I will never leave you and I will never abandon you." The success of our mission depends on the basis of this spritual truth.

More than rejoicing that the spirits obeying us, more than rejoicing that people are brought back from the dead, more than rejoicing in the transformation of the nations, we should really be rejoicing in the fact that our names are written in heaven.

The commandment to rejoice

But "rejoice in the Lord" is passed on to us as a commandment. It isn't a gentle recommendation: if you're in the mood for a little bit of rejoicing, then it'll be good to rejoice to cheer your heart, activate your brain and improve your immune system! No, the King of Kings himself *orders* us to rejoice!

Even though it's normal to only rejoice when we feel like rejoicing, if that was all there was to it, then we wouldn't need a commandment to tell us to rejoice. It's precisely because we get ourselves into situations where we don't feel like rejoicing that God gives us the commandment to rejoice. This is what makes it an act of obedience based on our faith. When Jesus commanded the man with a withered hand to stretch out his hand, (Matthew 12:13) he must surely have tried to stretch out his hand in the past but found that he didn't have any strength in it. Even though he was probably very disappointed after having had that experience any number of times, he decided that he would stretch it out one more time. Because it was none other than Jesus who told him to stretch out his hand, he stretched it out, because he believed that Jesus would surely heal him.

In the same way, the Lord says to us, "Blessed are you when people insult you and persecute you and say all kinds of evil things about you falsely on account of me. Rejoice and be glad because your reward is great in heaven." (Matthew 5:11–12) In the midst of trials and suffering, rather than trying to defend ourselves or retaliating, we rejoice because Jesus tells us to rejoice. In fact, we don't just rejoice, we rejoice and dance and celebrate, because it's in those times we can know that God is giving us a reward in heaven!

We can rejoice not because of what we see with our physical eyes, but because with the eyes of faith we can see Jesus on the cross for us, we rejoice because we can see with hope God who gives to us the glory of Christ. (see 1 Peter 4:12–13) In whatever situation, we rejoice because we know that we are yoked to Christ with a bond that cannot be broken, that we trust in a good and impartial judge, and that "we know that all things work together for good for those who love God." (Romans 8:28) I want to encourage you not to depend on your feelings or emotions but to exercise your will, bring yourself to obedience and always be rejoicing in your heart! (see 1 Thessalonicans 5:16)

Daily exercises in rejoicing

Paul taught the young Timothy that "physical exercise has some value, but godliness is valuable in every way." For example, stretches are one kind of physical exercise. When you first start, it might find it a hassle, but after a month of stretching every day you body will become really supple. In the same way, if you practice rejoicing every morning because your name is written in heaven, you'll naturally get into the pattern of rejoicing throughout your day-to-day life.

King David used to speak to his soul and put himself through this kind of spiritual training: "Praise the LORD, O my soul! With all that is within me, praise his holy name! Praise the LORD, O my soul! Do not forget all his kind deeds!" (Psalm 103:1-2) One evangelist I know, Yūichiro Nakano, uses David's training programme and has made it his daily practice. Every morning, he gets in front of a mirror and loudly declares, "Praise Him! Praise Him more! Praise Him as much as you can!"[1] I began to copy his practice, and as soon as I got up in the morning I would rejoice—perhaps sometimes getting a little over the top—that my name was written in heaven. This exercise is a bit like stretching out a muscle that has atrophied. As you continue to do it, you'd be amazed at how much joy begins to well up within you.

One lady had the same nightmare every night. In her dream, she was standing alone in a large field, and she found herself thinking, "Where do I go from here? What happens to me if I die?" At that point she used to wake up in horror, and wouldn't be able to get back to sleep. Once she'd gone through our training, from the very day that she got up in the morning and rejoiced that her name was written in heaven, she never had that same dream again and was able to sleep right through, and she was free from her fears about death and about the uncertainty of her future. She told me that after that, she started to evangelise and her friends came to believe in Jesus. The face of this lady as she testified was shining.

1 Yoshihiro Kishi, "JTJ Story, part 4", *JTJ News*, JTJ Missionary College. http://www.jesustojapan.com/jtjstory/jtjstory4.html (accessed April 09, 2010)

Upward, Outward, Inward

We start our Upward, Outward, Inward training with a song, and then next we teach a simple way of doing devotions. We teach two habits for people to get into as soon as they wake up in the morning so that they can have a one-to-one time of fellowship with God. The first is to express their joy before the Lord. In the training session itself, we do a Nakano-style "joy exercise." Then we get a progress report from them after a week and see how they're getting on.

The other thing we teach them is to have fellowship with God through six questions that they ask Him each morning. To do that, they need to be able to distinguish God's voice. In the next chapter, we'll look at how to do that.

If you get into the habit of "devoutly exercising" and lifting your eyes to Jesus in rejoicing every morning, you'll find that you quickly develop a rhythm of joy that fills your life.

5 Discerning God's Voice

Anyone can hear Him

When did you last hear God's voice?

When we talk about hearing God's voice, we don't mean actually hearing a physical voice with your physical ears. James tells us to "welcome the message implanted within you," (James 1:21) which suggests that God has already placed His words into our hearts. "Hearing God's voice" means accepting that message.

We are told to accept the words of God, and we are also told to watch over our hearts, guarding our hearts against words that are not the words of God, "for from it are the sources of life." (Proverbs 4:23) Hearing the voice of God is a totally fundamental skill for our personal growth, and for us to be able to carry out the works that God has commanded us to do.

So then, when do we hear God? Jesus said that "man does not live by bread alone, but by every word that comes from the mouth of God." (Matthew 4:4) The word "comes" there actually means "continues to come." For instance, when Jesus says, "Ask and it will be given to you," (Matthew 7:7) he's not telling you that you get three wishes and after that you're done. "Continue to ask and it will continue to be given to you" would better express God's unchangeable grace. So "comes from the mouth of God" doesn't mean something like "comes once a week when a spiritual leader expounds God's will to you." It means that words continually flow out of God's mouth for us. It means that God continually wants to be talking to us and in communion with us.

That continual longing of God is expressed beautifully in the Song of Songs: "O my dove, in the clefts of the rock, in the hiding places of the mountain crags, let me see your face, let me hear your voice; for your voice is sweet, and your face is lovely." (2:14) Just like in a close family where there's always a lot of talking going on, God always wants to be in conversation with us. It's that personal fellowship with God that revives us. God may well be always longing to talk to us, and His words may be the words of life for us, but how often do we miss those words by not listening?

I'd like to ask you one more thing. Who do you think can hear the voice of God?

When God likens his people to sheep, he wasn't saying that to praise us. Sheep are spectacularly cowardly animals. They are so timid that they can't even jump across a little stream by themselves. Of course, they don't have claws or fangs to attack an enemy. They've only got little legs and they're slow to run away, and they can't work as a team to defend themselves. They barely have the attentiveness, or the strategy, or the wisdom, to stay alive. But sheep do have one amazing ability. They can distinguish the voice of their shepherd. If they couldn't do that, they wouldn't survive very long at all.

Jesus, the good shepherd, "calls his own sheep by name and leads them out". (John 10:3) And these sheep—that is, his people—can distinguish the voice of God. Through the indwelling Holy Spirit, we are told that all believers can hear God's words to us. (see Acts 2:17–18)

Three knacks for hearing God's voice

The first "knack" to distinguishing God's voice is to consciously listen and pay attention to what He is saying. Someone who isn't listening to the voice of God might not believe that God wants to speak to them personally or that the sheep can hear the voice of the shepherd.

When God first spoke to Samuel, the young boy didn't understand what was going on. But when he said, "Speak, for your servant is listening," (1 Samuel 3:10) he was able to listen to God's voice. We start to hear God by standing on the promise that God is always speaking and that we have the ability to hear Him.

The second "knack" to distinguish God's voice is to not be afraid of getting it wrong. In Hebrews 5:14, it says that "solid food is for the mature, whose perceptions are trained by practice to discern both good and evil." If we're going to be able to taste some "meaty" spiritual food, rather than just spiritual milk and baby food, we need to practice refining our senses, not our intellects. Nobody has ever got onto a bicycle and managed to cycle off first time without ever falling over. You don't need a lot of intellectual knowledge to know how to ride a bike: sit on the saddle, point it the way you want to go, and pedal away. That's not the problem; the problem is not with the theory, but with the practice.

So how do we train our instincts? The answer is to make a lot of mistakes. If someone is so worried about making a mistake that they never get on a bike, then no matter how much they study about bikes, they're never going to be able to ride one. The way we train our instincts is through the process of not being afraid of our mistakes, and learn-

27

ing from our mistakes. If we later realise that we've heard God wrong, then we just pray "God, I'm sorry I heard you wrong. Please help me to get it right next time."

The third knack of hearing God is taking things a step at a time. Sometimes God speaks in a "soft whisper." (1 Kings 19:12) But the great thing is that as soon as we start to listen, we'll generally find that the words are already in our hearts, "for the one bringing forth in you both the desire and the effort–for the sake of his good pleasure–is God." (Philippians 2:13) As well as desire and effort in our hearts, there might also be fear, uncertainty, delusion and anxiety. We don't have to be disappointed when we recognise those things, because we know that "the human mind is more deceitful than anything else." (Jeremiah 17:9) We just need to ask ourselves what is the desire that God has brought forth in us.

Sometimes when we start we just won't know the answer, but if we become too cautious, we'll end up not getting any practice. Why not try holding what you think is God's will before Him, saying, "Lord, I think this is what you want me to do—is that right?" Speaking it out is a form of practice as well.

Next, after you've spoken it out, try checking whether or not it "feels right" with your own heart. If it feels wrong, then let it go and try again. Then inspect your heart again. If you then think "that was it," then try writing it down or talking with someone about it. This way you'll be able to work out whether or not you're being blown around by the wind. If it does "feel right" then pray: "Lord, I think this is what you want; if I'm going to accept this properly, then what should I do next?" As you search your feelings, you'll be able to tell whether or not this is a "headwind" or a "following wind": whether or not God supports your judgement.

It's important to keep repeating this process of weighing in your heart, believing that you can hear God and not getting too bogged down. As you pray, as you write, as you speak out, as you keep silence, your conviction will deepen, from "is it this?" to "it's probably this" to "I'm convinced it's this!"

The instructor's role

In the training, after a moment's silence, I say something like, "Please write down what's in your heart at the moment. After you write one thing, there'll be more things that come to you." Sometimes people write a huge swathe of things, sometimes people just struggle to come up with one. But usually everyone writes something. That's the first step of faith.

After that we get into groups of two or three and share the things that we think we've received, and pray for one another. At this point most people feel a peace about the guidance that they've received. Just like after someone manages to ride a few meters on a bicycle they then feel safe that they can try it on their own, people enjoy the experience of taking the plunge and bringing those messages that God has put inside them to their consciousness. That's the aim of the training.

The exercise is like when a batter makes a guess and works out what kind of ball is coming next. If he gets the ball that he expected, and he makes the swing that he's been practicing every day, he can enjoy making the hit that he has in mind. In baseball, someone who can do that on about a third of their trips to the plate is a great batter. The other two times, they get out. Similarly, when you start practicing hearing God's voice, it's good to relax, be generous to yourself and just try without worrying about what happens if you make a mistake. As you continue to practice, your batting average will go up!

It's through this process that God drills us so that we can better fight the fight of faith. The Lord "trains my hands for battle; my arms can bend even the strongest bow." (Psalm 18:34)

The role of the instructor is not, fundamentally, to teach the right way to hear, or to correct mistakes. If you notice things that can be affirmed and encourage people, then the things that are less desirable will naturally fade out over time.

I think the happiest person is the person who's just started on their walk of faith and is beginning to practice how to distinguish God's voice for themselves. No matter how much you practice, or how much experience you might have, you'll still occasionally make mistakes in hearing God, but if you start getting worried about your mistakes, you'll never come to hear God. All of us have a direct connection to God, and so all of us can hear His voice.

And let's not forget that it's Jesus who wants to talk to us every day. Our role is just to be courageous and open the door of our hearts to him. (See Revelation 3:20) I think that, to encourage us, Jesus will celebrate our first experiments.

If we keep practicing, learning from our mistakes, and maintain an attitude of learning from our mistakes, then surely we'll grow to hear His voice more and more accurately.

6 Questions for the Father

A two-way conversation

Have you ever had a phone call where the other person has barely given you any time to open your mouth, and as soon as they've said their piece, they put the phone down on you?

For a long time, that's how I used to pray.

As soon as I'd said the things that I wanted to say, I'd say, "Amen", just like I was slamming down the receiver, and the conversation between Jesus and myself would end. What a rude way to pray! Jesus never seemed to complain, but I'm sure he was thinking, "Listen to what I'm saying— just for a couple of minutes!"

Much of the time, we're like Martha—our heads filled with so many concerns. And yet the one thing that we really need to do in our lives is to "sit at the Lord's feet and listen to what he said" (Luke 10:39) So if we're going to have a conversation with God, what do we need to do? One good way to have a conversation with someone is to ask questions. So in our Upward, Outward, Inward training, every morning, just after our "expressions of joy," we recommend asking six questions to God.

Six questions every morning

First, we ask two questions about our Upward relationship. The first question is "Father, what do you think about me?" Once I did this training right in the south of Japan, and one of the attendees was a pastor. Before he started this exercise, he said that he was worried that God would say something very harsh to him. But after we tried it, he said, "I thought I was going to be told off, but He was so kind when He spoke to me; it was such a relief!" God has purchased us as His children through the death of His own son, and He has warm and loving things to say to us. He might say to you "my son, whom I love, with whom I am well pleased;" (Matthew 3:17) or maybe "you are precious and honored in my sight, and I love you;" (Isaiah 43:4) or perhaps "your voice is sweet, and your face is lovely." (Song of Songs 2:14)

God is so skilled at expressing His love for us, and we can enjoy hearing these expressions every morning. God loves you not because of what you might have done, but He loves you because you are His child.

The second question is "Father, what is it that you want me to do today?" Sometimes He'll draw your attention back to something that He's guided you about in the past and ask you to do the same again that day; sometimes He'll recommend that you start something new. Actually the reason I came to write this book is that one morning, the Father said, "I want you to write a book." Sometimes it'll be something which builds up our faith, such as "Don't worry about that thing, I'm taking care of it," or "What you're afraid of won't come to pass."

Sometimes when you're listening to the answer to the first question you'll also hear the answer to the second. For instance, it might go something like, "I've already made you a fountain of blessing, so today go to so-and-so's house and listen to what they have to say."

The third and the fourth questions relate to our Outward relationships, that is, the world around us. First, we ask "Today, who do you want me to serve, and how?" As it says in Ephesians 6:7, "obey with enthusiasm, as though serving the Lord and not people," and pray that you will be shown specifically who to serve, and in what way.

There are a lot of people who exploit and use other people in the world, but it's rare to find someone who serves others joyfully. Plenty of people want to talk about themselves, but it's rare to find someone who will sit quietly and listen to others. How many people, for instance, would continue to be a friend to someone even when it puts them at a disadvantage?

Jesus came as a guest to Zaccheus's house. All around us there are people who are thinking, "nobody needs me." We are called, as God's representatives, to go to those people, to pray peace upon them, (Genesis 12:2) to have a meal with them, (Luke 10:7) to meet their needs, (Matthew 25:31-46) to heal the sick, (Luke 4:18,19) and to "seek and to save the lost." (Luke 19:10)

The next question is, "Father, who can I be a witness to today, and what should I say?" If you're planning to meet someone that day who isn't a Christian, ask for a specific way to appeal to them. He may give you a short phrase that will be useful for you to share with them. For instance, even if you don't hear anything specific, you can still confirm what God's will is as soon as you get up in the morning; you can understand the mind of Christ who "had compassion on them because they were bewildered and helpless, like sheep without a shepherd." (Matthew 9:36)

The fifth and sixth questions are about your relationship with yourself and your friends. First, we pray, "Have

Upward, Outward, Inward

I committed any sins in the past 24 hours? Please bring me to repentance." According to Proverbs 28:13, "the one who covers his transgressions will not prosper, but whoever confesses them and forsakes them will find mercy." Examine yourself before God and confess any sins that He points out to you. This is how we are made clean and how we grow. The Father loves to develop us into "a mature person, attaining to the measure of Christ's full stature." (Ephesians 4:13)

Every day we check ourselves to see if we have fallen into sexual temptation, if we have used our finances, time, knowledge and gifts to God's glory, if we have murmured against God or other people, or if we have worked for the good of our neighbour. Where we have fallen short, we confess that before God.

Finally, we ask, "How should I show love to my fellow Christians or people in my mission team?" Paul teaches us to "be devoted to one another with mutual love, showing eagerness in honoring one another." (Romans 12:10) You'll often find a similar call to brotherly love at the end of each of Paul's epistles, and Jesus himself said that "Everyone will know by this that you are my disciples—if you have love for one another." (John 13:35)

People don't just see the acts of love that we do for them, but they also see the way we treat one another as Christians, and that's what attracts them to Christ. If we ask each morning how we can share love to a fellow believer, and if we then go and do it, this can be a powerful form of mission by itself.

Asking these questions of God every morning make up our "Upward Outward Inward devotions."

- Father, what do you think of me?
- Father, what is it that you want me to do today?
- Today, who do you want me to serve and how?
- Father, who can I be a witness to today, and what should I say?
- Have I committed any sins in the past 24 hours? Please bring me to repentance.
- How should I show love to my fellow Christians or people in my mission team?

Upward Outward Inward devotions

Questions throughout the day

If you start each day with these questions, it gets easier to stay in fellowship with God the whole day through. Jesus said, "I can do nothing on my own initiative. Just as I hear, I judge, and my judgment is just, because I do not seek my own will, but the will of the one who sent me." (John 5:30) Sometimes we can end up embarrassed when we realise that we're chasing our own hopes and dreams the whole time; instead, since we're also sent by the Father just like Jesus was, we should be leaving our own dreams to one side, dying to self, and seeking after the Father's heart every day.

So what questions should we ask as we go through our day? For example, when we're talking to someone, we might ask, "Father, teach me something about this person," and then listen to what God has to say. Sometimes we'll hear that the person we're talking to has some physical problem or illness. Other times He might tell us about a problem that someone is facing, or the way they see themselves in relation to others, or a part of His plan for their future. The reason He tells us this things is so that we can make it known to them how much God loves them. If we go through our day in conversation with God like this, we can discover new ways of introducing people to Jesus.

The other day, one lady made a chiffon cake. She ended up making too much, so she asked God, "Who should I give this cake to? Who should I take it around to?" Just then, the face of an old lady came into her mind, so she got on her bike and took the cake around to her. The old lady was so overjoyed when she received the cake that she cut off a quarter of it and shared that with a friend of hers who wasn't a Christian. This non-Christian lady said, "what a wonderful person it was that made this cake for you," and made a special effort to say thank-you to her.

This kind of evangelism isn't a programme, where you run a cake workshop every week; it's just a way of showing love to people as the Father guides you. I think that if ordinary people, with no special qualifications, start saying to God, "Please use me as your hands and your mouth," and following the guidance that He gives them, the world is going to be changed.

Even if we're listening to God, He doesn't always respond straight away, and sometimes even when He does, there are times when we misunderstand Him. But rather than not listen to Him at all and try to figure everything out for ourselves, there's a much more exciting way to live! If you continue this process, through trial and error, every day, then one day, you'll be able to hear and obey a very specific message like the one that Phillip received—"Get up and go south on the road that goes down from Jerusalem to Gaza." (Acts 8:26)

Start every day by having a conversation with God around these six questions. As you share in God's will, follow His directions and show love to other people, every day will be brimming with life!

7 | Upward Outward Inward Groups

Confess your sins to one another

I used to meet up with a teenage boy once a week; he was struggling to break the habit of accessing adult sites on his mobile phone. The youngster knew very well that this pornography addiction into which he had fallen was not pleasing to God. The first time that we met, he told me through his tears, "I want to stop. I really want to change." We prayed together that God would give him the power to overcome temptation, and then we met again a week later.

But when we met, he was still totally defeated; he'd been looking at the site every day. Once again, we prayed together about it. The next week, he told me that in the past week, there'd been one day when he hadn't look at the site. We gave thanks to God and rejoiced in that small step forward. Even though he was still doing it six times a week, that was still an important step in his growth.

The next week, he'd managed to resist temptation for two days: two wins and five losses. The next week, he was three-four down—I told him, "that's a better batting average than Ichiro!" After that, the number of days he resisted began to increase. Eventually, he was able to go a whole week without looking at any adult sites. He had decided to put a timer onto his phone to turn it off after nine o'clock at night, the time he was most liable to temptation. This was a wonderful experience for me as God bound us together: this young boy's fight became my fight, his victories became my victories.

John writes in 1 John 1:9 that "if we confess our sins, He is faithful and righteous, forgiving us our sins and cleansing us from all unrighteousness." Certainly if we recognise our failures and declare that God alone is righteous, then through that one to one relationship with Him, He will pardon us and purify us. But at the same time, James says that we should "confess your sins to one another and pray for one another so that you may be healed." (James 5:16) As we confess our sins to one another in the context of a loving and a supporting fellowship, the heart that has been bruised by sin can be healed, and we can receive the courage to overcome the power of sin.

Bible reading, intercession and sharing

In Upward Outward Inward training we confess our sins privately every morning, but each week, we also meet together in small groups to confess our sins to one another. We call these "Upward Outward Inward groups"; they're a modification of Neil Cole's Life Transformation Groups[1]. As well as confessing our sins, each week we share together about the good things that we've experienced in the week and all the things that are going on in our lives.

In these single-sex groups of about three people, meeting once a week for about an hour, we go through similar questions to the questions we use in the morning devo-

1   Neil Cole, *Cultivating a Life for God: Multiplying Disciples Through Life Transformation Groups*. Covina, CA: Churchsmart Resources, 1999

tions. When the group grows to four, we divide into two groups so that there's always two or three people.

The first two questions are Upward, about our relationship with God: "Looking back over the past week, when do you think that God was particularly with you?" "How has God been directing you through your Bible reading in the past week, and how have you put that into practice?"

The Outward questions, about our relationship with the world, and the Inward questions, about our relationship with ourselves and our Christian brothers and sisters, are pretty much the same as the questions from the morning devotions; it's a way of going over the things that we're working through every morning and sharing them with others: "This week, who have you served and in what way?" "In the past week, who have you shared the Gospel with and how?" "This week, have you committed sin?" "This week, what you have you done to show love to fellow Christians or to your mission team?" We confess our sins to each other, then pronounce 1 John 1:9 over each other, and receive forgiveness.

These groups don't have a leader; rather, as it says in Proverbs 27:17, "As iron sharpens iron, so a person sharpens his friend." Don't do this because you feel that you want to develop another person, but so that you yourself will be sharpened and developed through the fellowship; the other person will also be sharpened as a result. Discipleship will naturally happen as a result of a life of integrity and honesty, lived in fellowship with God and with your friends.

When these groups meet each week, each person answers each of the six questions. This is the "Inward" element of the groups. The "Upward" element is reading the Bible, and the "Outward" element is intercessory prayer together for non-believing friends and family. In this way, these groups form a simple discipleship system made up of

- Looking back over the past week, when do you think that God was particularly with you?

- How has God been directing you through your Bible reading in the past week, and how have you put that into practice?

- This week, who have you served and in what way?

- In the past week, who have you shared the Gospel with and how?

- This week, have you committed sin?

- This week, what you have you done to show love to fellow Christians or to your mission team?

Questions for Inward Upward Outward groups

"Upward", (Bible reading) "Outward" (intercession) and "Inward" (sharing) elements. The intercession and Bible reading parts are not done in the group time, but privately, at one's own pace. In the groups, we decide together which passage we're going to read and who we're going to pray for.

I want to explain the Bible reading element a bit more. Each week in our groups we decide to read between 25 and 30 chapters of Scripture. So for instance, Genesis has 50 chapters, so we might decide to read that over two weeks. Ephesians has six chapters, so we would read that five times in a week. First and Second Corinthians together have 29 chapters, so that's perfect for one week's worth. If someone in the group doesn't manage to get through the reading that we'd previously arranged, we don't go onto the next set of passages, but everyone does the same reading again; we keep reading the same set until everyone's read the whole lot. In these cases, don't harrass the person who hasn't read it all. Even if you have to read the same bit of the Bible many times over, take it to mean that the Holy Spirit wants you to learn a special lesson from that portion of Scripture.

Finally, the intercession. If you've got a group of three people, then each person should suggest two names of people that they'd like to see receive salvation; if it's a group of two people, then choose three people each. Either way you should end up praying for six people. Everyone then prays for one of those six people every day. This should mean that one non-Christian will have two or three people praying for them continuously, specifically and strategically over the course of a week. Because God hears our prayers, we can expect that person to come to faith. I study the Bible with about three or four businessmen every week, and each one of those people came to faith because they were prayed for by these Upward Outward Inward groups.

When these prayers are answered and someone comes to faith, a lot of the time they're going to start coming along to the Upward Outward Inward group the week later with the person who had been praying for their salvation, and either the group will divide or a two-person group will grow to become a three-person group.

Thirst and faithfulness come first

To help someone who's been a Christian for less than a week to be able to come along to these groups, we have a couple of unbreakable conditions. There's a separate kind of accountability group that's designed for cases where a husband and wife come to faith together, and we'll deal with that in the next chapter, but if someone who's already a Christian wants to join one of these groups, they must fulfill these two conditions.

First, they must be thirsty for more of Christ. It's important that they desire, above everything else, to be changed more into the likeness of Christ.

Upward, Outward, Inward

The second condition is that they submit themselves to faithfully following the process. Someone who is not prepared to keep their promises would be better off not joining in.

When I'm introducing these Upward Outward Inward groups to people, I tell them that only those who are both thirsty and faithful should come along. Sometimes pastors get the wrong end of the stick, and divide their whole congregation up into these groups. That just doesn't work. There's something like the eighty-twenty rule in operation, whereby, whenever you start something new, there's only about 20% of the people who will be really on board with it. People who want to maintain the status quo, or who feel obliged just to follow whatever their leaders tell them to do, are better off not joining in either.

I also don't think it's fair for leaders to suggest to others something that they're not prepared to do themselves; I think it's better for leaders to start off by praying together with a partner, starting an Upward Outward Inward group with them, and if they find that it changes their way of life, then add one person to that group. Or they could start on their own, pray that they'll find someone else who wants to start an Upward Outward Inward group and then pray for others to be saved so the group grows by dividing into two.

If you buy a bottle of really expensive mineral water, but you're not thirsty, then you're not going to drink it. People who aren't thirsty should wait until they're thirsty. Jesus said "If anyone is thirsty, let him come to me, and drink." (John 7:37) God seems to start off with a small number of catalytic people and through their living witness, makes all the people around them thirsty for Him. You have to make sure not to try to control this sort of grass-roots project, or otherwise you could end up losing that living relationship between man and God.

42

Also, if you're going to start something new, you may also have to give something else up. If you don't think about starting and giving up at the same time, then you won't be able to continue these groups for a long time; as the Chinese proverb says, if you chase two rabbits, you will lose them both.

Meeting once a week in small groups, checking each other to see if you're really living out Honour God and Love Neighbour, as well as reading the Bible every day and praying for non-Christian friends and relatives.

8 | Habits for Husbands and Wives

The family is important

If someone asked you what was the most important thing in your life, how would you answer? According to a 2008 survey by the Institute of Statistical Mathematics in Japan, the top answer would be "the family" at 46%[1]. In other words, most people think that the family is more important than life, health, themselves, and their material possessions. How did Japanese people come to have such a family-centered attitude?

Masahiro Tanaka, the author of "The Wandering Family,"[2] argues that after the second World War, nationalistic tendencies were blunted and the traditional village identity collapsed, and people's identities became relatively closely allied to their houses and families. Then at the end of the 90s, Japanese people devoted themselves to two dreams: the first was to own their own home; the second was to stay working at a high-earning job so

1   Institute of Statistical Mathematics, "The search for emotional contentment" *Press summary of the results of the 12th national character survey.* http://www.ism.ac.jp/kokuminsei/point.html (accessed April 09, 2010)

2   Masahiro Tanaka, *The Wandering Family: The rise and fall of the post-War family model.* Yuhikaku, 2005.

Upward, Outward, Inward

that their children could have a better education than themselves.

Now we've lost the economic basis to fulfil either of those dreams, neither individuals nor society really understand how to deal with the family, and so it is left, in Tanaka's words, "wandering." The Church can show Japanese society, and countries like it that are looking for a place of refuge and support, the way forward in relating to the family.

Three good habits

Let's hear from my friend Keishi. His view of the world used to be that the most important thing in life, and as a man, was to succeed at his work. So whenever he thought that his wife Kazumi was doing something or saying something that was a barrier to his "success," he would really tear into her. The relationship between him and his wife was more like the relationship between a boss and his worker.

One day Keishi's friend came to talk to him. This friend had just gone through a divorce, and said, "Looking at you, I feel like I'm looking at how I used to be; is your marriage doing OK?" Keishi was amazed when he heard this, because his understanding of the ideal marriage was a hard-working husband with an obedient wife. But after that, he and his wife came to see me together. I shared with him three good habits that myself and my wife had taken up.

These three good habits[3] are things for a couple to integrate into their daily routine. Special events to revive marriage relationships are like giving painkillers and sticking plasters to someone with a broken leg; they might work for a while, but they won't produce a lasting result. But

46

3   Taken from Douglas Weiss, *Intimacy: A 100-Day Guide to Better Relationships*, Lake Mary, FL: Siloam Press, 2001.

on the other hand, if we make showing love and honesty a part of everyday life, the feelings of longing and love for our spouse will naturally come back into flame and grow. A good relationship comes from being sincere and loving every day. What you sow in every day will determine what you reap. (Galatians 6:7–9)

So then, onto the three good habits.

The first habit is to share our hearts together and pray together.

> "Again, I tell you the truth, if two of you on earth agree about whatever you ask, my Father in heaven will do it for you. For where two or three are assembled in my name, I am there among them." (Matthew 18:19–20)

A couple can experience that promise by getting together, sharing their hearts together, and praying every day.

The second good habit is sharing our feelings. The skill of understanding how you feel and sharing that with your partner is something that can be trained and developed. As you polish up this skill you'll find it a lot easier to listen to one another and to accept each other. After praying for a short time, each person should go through what has happened to them in the past twenty-four hours, and how they've felt about that: whether it was emotional, lonely, afraid, sinful, lost, or whatever. Next, they should then remember the first time that they felt that kind of feeling and talk about that, and share experiences from their childhood or adolescence. The important thing here is that the spouse should not then immediately jump in with a similar story of their own, nor should they make any direct comment on the emotions that their spouse has expressed. The idea is to accept your partner just as they are, without judging them or trying to teach them something.

The third good habit is to warmly praise one other. Your spouse is the special person that God has selected just for you, and so is someone who is worthy of praise. We want to be encouraging our partner's growth, and praising them is the best way to do that. Every day, try and say two things that you like about your partner or that you're thankful for or something that they're great at. Don't feel self-conscious, but share wholeheartedly with one another. And when your partner praises you, just say "thank you" and move along; don't try to deny what they say, but accept it with thanks and store it up in your heart.

Let's go back to the story of Keishi and Kazumi. Some days later, Keishi said to me, "Through these habits that you've taught us, I've been able to accept my own wounds and weaknesses, and I've also come to understand my wife's pain and troubles. One day, God said to me, 'I created you so that you can shoulder Kazumi's burdens with her.'" Kazumi told me, "I was surprised myself to find that I had so many emotions going on inside me. I also began to notice so many things about my husband. The more I understood, the more the friendship between us developed. It feels like we've fallen in love all over again! Even our children have changed and they're behaving themselves a lot better as well."

Establishing a new model family

As Christian families take on these three habits, they'll be able to present this country with a new model for the family. Repaired and restored family relationships can be a model for intimate community that is not based on the premise of a secure job or a high salary, and can form a "window" for introducing people into the Kingdom of God, bringing thirst and admiration to a country and a society which is full of dysfunctional families.

The restored family is the most powerful weapon we have for evangelism. Non-Christian families can come to faith through being in contact with these family relationships, and, by taking on the three habits for themselves, they can form a continuous chain of testimony to others. That chain is not something that we bring about by raising up teachers or writing textbooks, but it's a movement that belongs to ordinary husbands and wives.

The church of the New Testament was a family church, and in it, family and church were united. The Old Testament is the same. People only worshipped at the Jerusalem Temple three times a year, and Israel's religion was based upon the family fellowship that took place every Sabbath[4]. Men who worked in farming or fishing or livestock rearing were sometimes unable to finish work in the evening and had to stay out overnight, but they would always come home by sundown on Friday. Then they would listen to their wives, gather around the meal that their wives had prepared, and teach their children the words of the Lord. (see Deuteronomy 6:7–9)

These days, the restoration of the family is an important issue but the real root of the problem is that the family has become separated from the church. We do not need another dualistic solution, such as running family seminars in our churches, but we need to take the view that the family *is* the church, and that the restoration of the family can change the world[5].

The "three habits" are Upward Outward Inward groups for the family. Prayer is the Upward element; setting an infectious example to other families is the Outward element; and sharing our feelings and praising each other is the Inward element. People who come to faith as a

4   Marvin R. Wilson. *Our Father Abraham: Jewish Roots of the Christian Faith*, Grand Rapids, MI: Wm. B. Eerdmans, 1989.

5   Mitsuo Fukuda, "A New Family Model for Japanese People." In *Family and Faith in Asia: The Missional Impact of Social Networks.* edited by De Neui, Paul H., Pasadena, CA: William Carey Library, 2009.

couple can start this straight away as a couple-centered Upward Outward Inward group.

Practice showing emotions

The "three habits" are also a way of training us to recognise and express our emotions. Humans are thinking beings, but we're also feeling beings. Our emotions, like our intelligence, are a fundamental part of our personality, created by God so that we could express them to others. So when we surpress our emotions, fight against them, gloss over them or contain them, then we're living in a way that ignores an important domain of the life that God has given us. Many of our modern problems are due to the fact that we try to adjust ourselves to social models of rationality and co-operation, and as a result we end up not knowing what it is that we are really feeling.

But our emotions are necessary things. Understanding what we feel, feeling it as it really is, and appropriately expressing it to others, helps us to understand ourselves and to understand our partner. Try getting to grips with these habits to build up the skill of showing your emotions. Maybe it's useful for you to have a list of emotions so that you can identify what's going on inside you. Look for a different emotion every day and express it, and it will deepen the understanding between you and your partner and bring you closer together.

Out of the great variety of human relationships, the Bible chooses the husband-wife relationship to define the relationship between Christ and his Church. (Ephesians 5:21,23) One part of "loving your wife as your own body" (Ephesians 5:28) is listening every day to understand what sort of emotions she is carrying around and living with. On top of this, it's actually enjoyable, because through it you can be sure of the deep connection you have together.

Finally, through talking with your spouse, you can imagine how much Christ rejoices to hear your own private thoughts.

Let's have a look at some of the words you might find helpful to describe your own inner life: fun, joy, fear, dread, anger, sadness, shame, worry, sorrow, happiness, bliss, doubt, confusion, nostalgia, yearning, mourning, pining, closeness, respect, regret, bitterness, hate, loathing, repugnance, peace, safety, thankfulness, discontent, surprise, curiosity, desire, ambition, courage, pride, relaxation, superiority, inferiority, resignation, disappointment, pain, need, expectation, emptiness, contempt, jealousy, anxiety.

When husbands and wives pray together, share their feelings together, and praise each other, the family will be restored and will become a window through which to introduce others to the Kingdom of God.

9 Winning With Your Story

You are already the light of the world

When Jesus went to a town called Gesara, he met a man there with many demons, and Jesus drove the demons out of him. After a series of confusing events, the man begged Jesus to let him become one of Jesus's followers, but Jesus said to him, "Return to your home, and declare what God has done for you." (Luke 8:39) He went home and shared his experience. I'm sure it must have gone something like this: "I used to run around naked in the tombs, causing all kinds of trouble, but this man called Jesus came and drove the demons out of me. Look at me now, I'm back to normal! Surely this is a miracle, surely this is of God!"

Some time after this man had shared what had happened to him, we're told that "large crowds followed Jesus" from that area, the Decapolis. (Matthew 4:25) God used someone who used to be a nuisance to all those around him to bring salvation to a wide area, the ten towns around his home town of Gesara.

I think this shows us that God quite happily uses people who have "only just got saved." Every believer is already "the light of the world," (Matthew 5:14) and so we shouldn't be trying to hide that light; rather, we should be going out amongst people who don't believe yet and helping them to worship their heavenly Father. If someone who comes to faith doesn't deliberately get themselves back out into the world, within three years, all of their friends will be Christians. But someone who's only just become a Christian has already a whole host of personal connections with non-Christians, and so is already a much better point of contact with the rest of the world. We shouldn't allow this kind of opportunity to slip away!

Jesus comes to live in someone as soon as they turn to him. If we say that new Christians can't witness until they've studied correct doctrine and their personality has matured, then we're underestimating the Lord of the mission. Let's not look down upon Christ; he already resides within new believers.

To be honest, I was much better at witnessing when I was a new Christian than I am today. I might have spent an awfully long time studying "right doctrine" but many more people came to faith through me when I was a new Christian than they do now. I think that's because people now can't see the life-transforming change that happened to me at the time.

Making an outlet for grace

Even if you think from the point of view of their long-term discipleship, it's important for people to have the experience of evangelizing straight after they come to faith.

The grey goose chick, right after it's born, takes the first thing that it sees and hears as its mother; this is called "imprinting." Christians also quite often take the first Christian that they meet and the first teaching they receive after they've been saved as the model for their Christian life from then on. There's a saying that "the child is father to the man," and that's especially the case for spiritual children: who they are at the start of their spiritual journey determines the course of their walk with God. If they're pointed in the right direction in the first 48 hours of their Christian life, that will determine the outcome from then on.

One of my friends, the day after he came to faith, was helped by the person who brought him to Christ to go and witness about his salvation to someone else. At the time, he thought that it was a very exciting and a very important thing to do, and even today he's evangelizing pretty much every day. I wonder how many people have found the way to new life through his testimony.

The most important thing for new believers to do is to secure an outlet for grace. If you teach people that they shouldn't evangelise until they're healed, cleaned up, matured and filled with the Spirit, then they'll become passive and miss out on experiencing the joy of sharing with others. Healing and purification and maturation are things that you have to deal with all the way through your life, so if you wait until that's all finished, you're never going to get out there! According to the writer to the Hebrews, someone with bad legs needs "straight paths for your feet" (Hebrews 12:13) as much they need healing and rehabilitation. In a lot of cases, people will be gradually healed and purified and matured through the process of "Honor God, Love Neighbor" anyway.

Similarly, if you over-emphasise the idea that before you evangelise you have to be filled with the Spirit, people tend to become inward-looking. But if you tell people to "Go into all the world and preach the gospel to every creature," (Mark 16:15) and they go out and do it, then they will "know at once that power had gone out" from them. (Mark 5:30)

One lady was evangelizing someone who had a real fear of dying. So she explained how, if you believe in Jesus, he

55

will give you eternal life, and they prayed together, and after that this person felt safe and began to seek after Jesus for themselves. As a result of this, the lady who was doing the witnessing herself also changed. It turns out that she herself had also had a fear of dying, and through the process of testifying to Jesus' resurrection, she found that her own fears were being dealt with. As the Holy Spirit flows "Outward" to others, it also washes us and changes us "Inward."

How to evangelize

There are many ways to share the Gospel, but the starting point of all of them is the mission heart of God. God is asking "Whom will I send? Who will go on our behalf?" If we hear that and say "Here I am, send me!" (Isaiah 6:8) then God will show us each and every time who to speak to and what approach to use.

But there are some principles. One is to become such a true friend to the other person that they know that we're understanding them as they really are. God himself loves that person, and so we, as God's hands and feet in that situation, are to show His love to them. Try to hear their story from their own point of view, understand their needs, help them with anything concrete that would be useful to them, and deepen your relationship with them; serve them joyfully as you seek God's direction for them. Sometimes to be a good friend you'll need to ask them for help as well, just like Jesus did in asking the Samaritan women for a drink of water.

Another principle is to think about how you can use the resources that you have available to help your friend's community whilst still respecting the authority figures within the community. As you get closer to them, boldly hold them up in prayer. Of course, you could offer to pray for someone as soon as you meet them, if God leads you to do that. In my experience, if you say to someone, "Is it OK if I pray for you?" then most people will not refuse. I think God can bring about healings and miracles to show a non-Christian His power and His love.

Sometimes it's good to have a short phrase which expresses the relationship between you and God, to help you discern those who are thirsting for the truth. Something like "I think I'm really blessed; maybe it's because God loves me" which you can say fairly naturally. Ask God to show you in your morning devotions how to say this sort of thing.

Of course, more often than not, you'll be given the words you need to say at the time. If we obey God's guidance when we're out on the mission field, then God can bring salvation to the household, like He did with the house of Zaccheus in Jericho in Luke 19:1–10—or to the town, like He did with the town of Sychar in John 4:3–42—or to the whole country, like He did with Ethiopia through the eunuch in Acts 8:26–40.

But no matter who we come into contact with, we should recognise Christ in "one of the least of these brothers or sisters of mine" (Matthew 25:40) and serve them motivated by pure and unexaggerated love. If the other person is open to faith then we can lead them into eternal life, but even if not, there are still good reasons to love them. We were sent to serve people in the same way that Jesus did.

90 Second Testimonies

If someone responds to our actions in serving them, or the miracles that they've seen happen in God's name, or our short phrase about our relationship with God, then what do we do? When that happens, be like the man from Gesara and tell your own story.

In Upward Outward Inward training, we train people how to share their testimony with their neighbor as soon as they come to faith, because we're commanded to "always be ready to give an answer to anyone who asks about the hope you possess." (1 Peter 3:15) There are three points to the training.

The first is to have something which clearly shows a before/after. We practice explaining in 90 seconds what their situation was before they came to faith, how they met Jesus, and how they changed after that. This is so people can understand the big picture of what God has done.

The second point is to use one verse from the Bible. Our lives are a "letter of Christ" (2 Corinthians 3:3) that God has written. As we tie our experiences to the Bible, then the person we're talking to can "acknowledge the Lord," (Proverbs 3:6) and at the same time we can plant the seed of the Word in their hearts.

Thirdly, we want them to imagine the person that they're talking to worshipping God. So don't go on and on with a difficult story, or say something like "I looked and then I found," taking the credit for God's work for yourself. Pray while you talk that your joy will be transferred into the other person's heart.

In our training sessions themselves, we get into groups of two and practice evangelizing to one another. In one place we did it, we trained a man in the morning in how to give a 90 second testimony, and in the lunch break he led two young men to faith. Since God has prepared people for us, let's not let these kinds of situation pass without doing anything. Don't be afraid of failure, but give it your best shot.

Lots of people tell me that mission in this country is difficult. But Jesus said that "the fields are already white for harvest" (John 4:35) There are people waiting to hear your testimony. (see Acts 16:9,10; 2 Timothy 4:2) Keep sharing your testimony until it becomes another part of your lifestyle!

Just so that you know, there's a difference between testimony and argument. I'm not suggesting that you try to win people over with your words. Francis of Assisi said, "Preach the gospel at all times; if necessary, use words." It's not enough for your testimony to depend on your words; more than anything, the way that you live will be the message. A life of loving your neighbor is the most powerful way of sharing the Good News.

When someone who's only just become a Christian serves others out of love and starts to share the Gospel with them, God can do amazing things, and the new Christian themselves will grow at the same time.

10 Managing Your Money

A little clothes shop

Once upon a time, a man went home to the country and started up a little clothes shop. His friends were all against the idea, saying, "How can someone as quiet as you run a sales business?" But he replied, "God has told me to do this, so it will be fine."

He gave 20% of his profits to God, and he had a short time of worship with his employees every morning so that they would put Jesus first in their work. Soon he found that sales had taken off so much that people were lining the streets in front of his shop. Two major supermarkets came to the neighborhood, but he prayed that God would protect his business, and both shops moved away, allowing him to continue with his little clothes shop. He and his family would all evangelise together, and many people in that town came to faith.

What's the point of money?

No one can serve two masters, for either he will hate the one and love the other, or he will be devoted to the one and despise the other. You cannot serve God and money. (Matthew 6:24)

There are people who really love money as if it were their god. There are some people who serve money as if they were serving a god. But to put your trust in money is to distrust God, who has prepared all things for us to enjoy. Solomon knew this danger, and prayed, "do not give me poverty or riches; feed me with my allotted portion of bread." (Proverbs 30:8) The most important thing is how we use the money that has been entrusted to us. We've been sent out into this world like children who have been sent on an errand; Jesus said, "Just as the Father has sent me, I also send you." (John 20:21) God rejoices greatly at the work that we do with Him in the world.

But as well as sending us out, God has prepared two things for us: instructions and resources. Those are the things that He is responsible for preparing. The "instructions" are the principle of Honor God Love Neighbor living, and the instruction to fill the world with Honor God Love Neighbor living. One of the resources for that is money. "And my God will supply your every need according to his glorious riches in Christ Jesus." (Philippians 4:19) God gives us money for His glory and to bless our neighbors. It's not the meaning of our lives, but its means.

Principles for managing money

Let's break down the principles for handling our money in the familiar three ways: Upward, Outward and Inward.

I would suggest that the "Upward" element is that we can have fellowship with God through donating to his work. Donations are "a fragrant offering, an acceptable sacrifice, very pleasing to God." (Philippians 4:18) When we give away money, we are not thinking about our own convenience, but remembering that God has given us life. Giving a proportion of our income is a way to show love, respect and thanks to God. But of course we cannot donate to try to manipulate or bribe God.

Even if we gave all of our income, that would not be too much, (See 1 Chronicles 29:14) but "to every man whom God has given wealth, and possessions, he has also given him the ability to eat from them, to receive his reward and to find enjoyment in his toil." (Ecclesiastes 5:19) God rejoices in seeing me rejoice. So we can show our thanks to God by living a simple life with the income we receive, enjoying our work and giving back the rest of our money to the God who has given us everything in the first place.

In fact, if we think that we're going to give money if we happen to have any left over, then we're missing a chance to give. "But above all pursue his kingdom and righteousness, and all these things will be given to you as well." (Matthew 6:33) Instead, when money comes in, let's decide how much we're going to give and set that aside. (see 1 Corinthians 16:2) "God loves a cheerful giver." (2 Corinthians 9:7) Let's give cheerfully and enjoy the fellowship with God it provides.

The "Outward" element is that we use the money that we've saved for apostolic purposes. How should we use that money that we've regularly set aside? Should we have a democratic discussion and a vote on it? Or should we use it prophetically, dispensing it as we are led? One clue is the verse in Acts 4:35 where people brought their wealth, "placing them at the apostles' feet."

The word "apostles" means "those who are sent," those who are sent out to fill the earth with the Good News, building a foundation for the discipling movement. "Placing it at the apostles' feet" means first supporting apostolic teams (see Ephesians 4:11) as they are sent out to the various churches on the mission field. But of course at the time there was no such thing as "full time Christian workers" supported by regular offerings and gifts. Instead, "the proceeds were distributed to each, as anyone had need." (Acts 4:35)

Secondly, money should be used to expand discipleship projects into new areas. Sometimes we give out a one-time donation to local leaders and elders, or to support travel expenses for candidates in apostolic teams. (See 1 Timothy 5:17)

The third way to use money to support those in need within the community of faith. If you give out money fairly with this motive in mind, then there should be "no one needy among them." (Acts 4:34)

When you decide which of these ways to use your money, you could talk together, or you could look for prophecy, but the principle of using it for apostolic purposes has to be the basis of that process.

The "Inward" element is a warning against being too attached to money. One way to catch a monkey is to make a hole big enough for the money to get its hand into, but not big enough for it to get its fist through. If you put some food in the hole, the monkey will reach in to take it, make a fist, and won't let go of the food. It will be caught by its own greed. In the same way, those who grasp for money will fall into its grasp. If you can't let go of money, then you will become its servant.

> For the love of money is the root of all evils. Some people
> in reaching for it have strayed from the faith and stabbed
> themselves with many pains. (1 Timothy 6:10)

As it says in Hebrews 13:5, "Your conduct must be free from the love of money and you must be content with what you have." We need to regularly check ourselves to see if money is likely to be a temptation to us. Try to encourage those who just come to faith to make their first donation and decide to commit to regular giving. Giving up your money is an important step on the road to giving up your whole life for God. "For where your treasure is, there your heart will be also." (Matthew 6:21)

Back to Business

I run a small business myself. The other day I had lunch with the owner of a nearby business. I asked him how business was going, and he said, "Well, you know this economic climate... I'm just treading water. But your company seems to be doing well, doesn't it? Probably the best of any of them around here." I instantly replied, "Our boss has got it worked out; the boss of our company is Jesus!" My friend looked surprised. "What do you mean? Are you are Christian?" I nodded, and he continued. "Ah, I thought so. Last month when we met at the chamber of commerce meeting I felt there was something unusual about you. I can't say what it was but I definitely felt something. That's why I thought I wanted to meet up and have a chat with you."

After that I was able to witness to him about how Jesus had guided and protected our business. He then told me that he'd like to introduce me to another friend. "I've known Mr X since we were children, but he's having a few problems at the moment. I think it'd be great if he became a Christian. I'll introduce you sometime." Paul recommended that "whether you eat or drink, or whatever you do, do everything for the glory of God." (1 Corinthians 10:31) I take that to mean that we should be reflecting the glory of God even in our business life.

In our society, there are more than a few businesses which quietly have connections with new religions or fortune tellers. To varying degrees, they consult with their objects of worship to entreat them for the prosperity of the business. But the Christian businessperson has the ability to call on the owner of the whole world for wisdom and power, and to apply these things to their work. God will receive the glory by making this difference obvious to people.

The world of business has a huge influence on the society as a whole. The value structures and patterns of thinking that you see in the business world will impact upon many different corners of society; an obvious example are the number of dysfunctional families with workaholic or absentee fathers. Diligence and originality in business are wonderful things in themselves. But at the same time, we need to learn the value of loving our neighbors, supporting our families, and looking to establish a spirit of righteousness, justice and mutual support within our communities and our country.

When ordinary Christians experience the power and love and wisdom of Jesus in their workplaces, and turn that into a testimony, then the business world itself can become a tool in God's hands. As Christian business people seek that "even now as always, Christ will be exalted in my body, whether I live or die" (Philippians 1:20) then they can use the financial resources that God has given them for the purposes of His kingdom.

We can be free from our attachment to money by managing the money that God has given us according to kingdom purposes, using it for the glory of God and the blessing of our neighbors.

11 Interactive Bible Studies

One summer vacation, six students had been playing together all afternoon. In the evening, they decided to study the Bible together. The passage that they'd chosen was Romans chapter 6.

After they'd read it out, one verse each, they shared together what they'd learnt from the passage. But in that passage there were a whole host of new ideas that they didn't understand. After a moment of silence, one of the high school students opened his mouth. "When it talks about the old man and the new man, what does that mean?"

There was another moment of silence. Then the student who was acting as the facilitator remembered something that had happened that same day. "I think it's something like this. At lunchtime, Ken and Ichiro had a fight. Then Ken said, 'hey, leave me alone.' The 'old man' is the sort of person who, when Jesus says something to him, goes 'hey, leave me alone'. And just like Ken and Ichiro made up afterwards, the 'new man' says sorry to Jesus and makes up." When they heard that, the other five students nodded their heads and said, "yeah, that's right."

Now if there had been a theologically-trained adult in with that group, they would probably have come out with some perfunctory explanation, using all kinds of jargon like reconciliation and sanctification and imputed and imparted righteousness. But as it was, these boys were interpreting the Bible out of their own experience and in their own words. That's the main point of the kind of study that we're going to introduce in this chapter. When we trust Jesus's instructions that we should "not be afraid, little flock" (Luke 12:32) and leave things to him, then amazing things can happen; there is no better Bible teacher than the Lord Jesus himself.

One of the things that's essential for a daily walk with Christ is that anyone should be able to learn directly from the Bible. Of course there are going to be difficult and obscure passages, but even learned theologians have spent many years arguing over such passages and haven't come to any agreement. On the other hand, if you read it in an honest attitude of seeking the truth, you can probably understand God's heart clearly from about 98% of the Bible, even if you're not a learned theologian.

I'm very thankful of the hard work of theologians in trying to interpret the Bible, and I've learnt a lot myself from their works, but the most important thing for the discipling of the whole world is the extent to which ordinary people can read and understand the Bible and then go on to put its words into practice. We are all called to be priests to one another, "teaching and exhorting one another." (Colossians 3:16) That means that even if someone isn't a religious specialist, they can learn all kinds of things from the Bible and through honest conversations where they reflect upon their lives and apply what they've learnt. And someone who's had a problem and obeyed what they've learnt from the Bible can be an encouragement to others with the same sort of problem through their living testimony.

Listen to it, carry it out, share it

I want to share another example with you. I used to really love preaching. I loved the feeling, when I was preparing a sermon, that I was in relationship with God and being directly taught the truth by Him. I loved being able to share that truth that had come out of a deep relationship with God. Sometimes I used to think "today's sermon was a work of art," and I'd get myself puffed up with self-praise and pride. But I had a problem. Even though the people who were listening to these 'fantastic' (?) sermons told me that they could understand them very clearly, their lives were not being changed!

After preaching one sermon, an old man said to me, "Pastor, you're young, you can say these things, but in reality it's not that easy. The Bible might say such-and-such, but I can't do that!" Well, I started seeing that pattern everywhere—people may well be coming to faith, but at the same time, when I spoke to people like that old man, I realized my failure. So after a while I stopped preaching and instead changed to a style of worship where we all studied the Bible together.

At the time, we'd read Bible passages together one verse each, and then we had the rule that each person made a comment on the passage that they'd read. One lady had read John 9:41:

> Jesus replied, "If you were blind, you would not be guilty
> of sin, but now because you claim that you can see, your
> guilt remains."

The lady who had read that passage said, "I used to think that I could see, but I couldn't see. I'm a sinner." The place was filled with emotion. I glanced up at her face; it was stained with tears. From that day onwards, her lifestyle totally changed. She had been taught by the Bible itself and obeyed God through its word.

That's when I realized that the Bible can speak directly to individuals. I understood that my role was not to place myself between God and man, but to help people to stand before God for themselves. We call our Bible study groups "interactive Bible studies," because they don't involve one person teaching the Bible and everyone else sitting around listening; everyone participates and is involved in the discussion.

How to hold an interactive Bible study

Let's have a look at how these interactive Bible studies work. There are various ways of doing it, but I'm going to introduce you to the one that works for me.

First, we need a facilitator. That's something that everyone takes it in turn to do. The facilitator for a study needs to choose a passage of between three and ten verses. Then they choose someone to pray for three things: first, that we will be able to hear God's voice speaking through this passage; second, that we'll be able to put those things into practice; third, that we'll be able to share those things that we've learnt and things that we've decided to do with other people.

Next, we either read the passage silently, or someone reads it out. Then we are silent for a few minutes. We repeat this pattern of reading and keeping silence. Then, before the second or third reading, the facilitator will say, "After this, we're going to get into pairs, and then choose one thing to share with the group." Then after a moment of silence, we get into pairs and each person shares with their partner three things: what we've learnt, how we're going to put it into practice, and how we're going to share it with someone else after the group. Just before we get into pairs, the facilitator says, "You're going to share what your partner said, so please pay good attention to them."

Then, when they think that both partners have finished sharing, they say, "Now, check that you've properly understood what your partner has told you; say something like 'I think you're saying such-and-such; is that right?'"

And then when everyone is ready, each person shares with the group in turn the things that their partner talked about. Then when everyone has finished, people discuss the contents. There are three things we're looking for in this time: first, that someone feels that what they've heard is definitely from God because someone else heard the same thing; second, that someone didn't realize something that someone else said, and so they've learnt something; third, that God seems to be saying something to the whole group. Finally, we get back into pairs and pray together that we'll be able to put into practice what we've learnt from the Bible.

Even someone who has only just become a Christian or someone who has only just started studying the Bible regularly can act as a facilitator. Even if there's someone there who raises difficult questions, the facilitator is just there basically to direct the traffic; they don't have to answer the question themselves but can pass it on to someone else. If the facilitator starts to control everything themselves, they rob everyone of the chance of studying together. If it happens that nobody there can answer the question, you can decide on someone who will go away and find out before next time. But the point of the Bible study is not that we come away knowing more about the Bible; it's that each person can be taught directly by God from the Bible, (Upward) that we can all follow God as we go out into the world, (Outward) and that we can encourage one another. (Inward)

If we believe in the priesthood of all believers, then everyone can learn God's will together through interaction with

Upward, Outward, Inward

the Bible, put it into practice in their daily lives, and encourage one another.

Only read on if you've put this into practice

So far we've introduced seven skills: a lifestyle of listening and obeying, devotions, Upward-Outward-Inward groups, habits for married couples, personal evangelism, management of finances and interactive Bible studies. Our training is actually like a two-storey building, and only those who have put into practice six out of the seven skills go on to the second part of the training, the second storey: you can choose either one of Upward-Outward-Inward groups or the habits for married couples, although of course it's great to do both!

Previously I didn't separate out the two 'storeys' and just taught everyone the whole lot in one go, but that caused two problems. First, we covered too many subjects in the training sessions and the focus got a bit blurry. But also there was no way of telling if people had actually gone on to put these things into practice!

After Jesus had sent out the disciples he took the time to listen to the results of their labors. (See Luke 10:17–24) When he saw that people had reached a certain level, he recognized the grace that had got them to that point and gave thanks. And the disciples had the opportunity to share what they'd learnt from their experiences and any problems that they'd had out on the field, and he was able to teach them. If you teach people who haven't actually gone out and done it for themselves, you end up raising up a lot of people who have knowledge but don't obey. Just sticking people into seminar after seminar does them no good and much harm. So we just choose the things that someone will need in the first two days after coming to faith, and then we can tell whether or not they can put those things into practice.

73

Upward, Outward, Inward

What we've taught in the first storey is the answer to the question "how should I live?"; the second storey deals with "how should I train others and send them out?" I don't normally give out the materials for the second storey until I've seen that people have managed to digest the topics of the first, but in this book, so that you can understand the whole picture, we'll just go up the stairs a little and see what the second storey looks like.

12 ■ Sending Out Disciplers

The 2-2-2 principle

If I asked you how many disciples Jesus had, how would you respond? Twelve is probably the number that first comes to mind. But then it says in Luke 10:1 that "the Lord appointed seventy-two others and sent them on ahead of him two by two into every town and place where he himself was about to go."

So how did he disciple those seventy-two? I'm guessing, but I wonder if he entrusted the discipleship of these seventy-two others to his Twelve. The Twelve would have operated in six two-man teams. If each of those six teams had twelve people to disciple, that's seventy-two people. Jesus intended to hand over the baton of discipling to the next layer of leader/disciplers. This corresponds with what Paul commanded to Timothy to "entrust what you heard me say in the presence of many others as witnesses to faithful people who will be competent to teach others as well." If we count from Paul's teacher, Barnabas, then we see the baton of discipleship passing down the generations from Barnabas to Paul to Timothy to "faithful people" to "others as well." We call this principle of exponential multiplication in discipleship the "2-2-2 principle", from the verse 2 Timothy 2:2.

So what did these seventy-two people do with the baton of discipleship that they had received from the Twelve? They were also sent out in two-man teams; that is to say, thirty-six discipling teams were sent out all through Israel. If we imagine that each of those teams raised up twelve people in the same way that they were discipled in a group of twelve, then you have $36 \times 12 = 432$ people.

We're told that after the risen Jesus met Peter and the Twelve, "then he appeared to more than five hundred of the brothers." (1 Corinthians 15:6) If you add the 72 that were sent out to the 432 people that they discipled, then you get just over 500 people who would have been in Jerusalem for the festival.

Now if all of these 500 people were sent out in two-man teams then we have 250 discipling teams, and if they could reach twelve people each, they would be able to disciple $250 \times 12 = 3000$ people. This tallies with the time that Peter preached on Pentecost and "that day about three thousand people were added." (Acts 2:41) When those three thousand were saved, there were already teams of people prepared who were able to disciple them.[1]

The virus of the Kingdom

I don't think it's a problem whether or not the numbers we've just given are strictly accurate, but I think what we can assume, when we look at disciples growing sixfold by sixfold from 12 to 72 to 500 to 3000, is that the principle is not one of addition but one of multiplication.

1   See David S. Lim, "Towards a Radical Contextualization Paradigm in Evangelizing Buddhists." In *Sharing Jesus in the Buddhist World*. Edited by Lim, David and Steve Spaulding. Pasadena, CA: William Carey Library, 2003. pp. 75-76.

Paul was called a "pest" by the Jewish authorities (see Acts 24:5) but perhaps we could say in more modern language that he was someone with a power that was as contagious as a cold! People who were "touched" by Paul's lifestyle and his teaching became converts and were discipled and then started a chain where they went on to disciple others. As a result, the whole area was filled with disciples, spreading like an infection. The "virus of the Kingdom" spreads from person to person, breaking down barriers of country and people group and culture. It's essential that we see chains of discipling start in order to fulfil the Great Commission.

Elephant churches and rabbit churches

We can divide churches into two types, if we think about their speed of reproduction: there are rabbit churches, and there are elephant churches. An elephant has four reproductive cycles a year, and gestation takes 22 months. In each cycle, there is at most one elephant born, and an elephant does not reach sexual maturity until the age of 18. If the conditions are right, elephants reproduce at the rate of about one every three years.

Rabbits, on the other hand, don't exactly have set reproductive cycles, gestation takes a month, and there are on average seven rabbits in a litter. Baby rabbits reach sexual maturity after four months. In three years, one breeding pair of rabbits can produce a family numbering, according to one calculation, four hundred and seventy-six million[2].

Elephant churches tend to have a single salaried leader who is an expert preacher and builds a solid church through planning and carrying out evangelism—which tends to

2   Wolfgang Simson, *The House Church Book: Rediscover the dynamic, organic, relational, viral community Jesus started*. Carol Stream, IL: Tyndale, 2009, p.58.

mean inviting people into the church building. On the other hand, rabbit churches are a family-style fellowship with every member directly connected to God, teaching each other how to live out Honor God, Love Neighbor in their ordinary lives, and being sent out to transform their communities.

If we redefine "church" as being "a small group for discipleship and mission", then we can get much closer to the idea of the priesthood of all believers. I've seen cases where housewives and students and office workers and shop workers have stepped out of the framework of building-centered clergy-crafted programmes, lead their friends and family to the Lord and discipled them, and saw a rabbit-church grow to five generations.

Please don't misunderstand me. I'm not saying that rabbit churches are the be all and end all. Rabbit churches have a danger of falling into heresy, just like elephant churches do. This is a universal danger that all of God's people must fight against, no matter what style of church they are part of. But I believe that the risk is smaller in rabbit churches, where there's an environment in which everyone is able to speak out and everyone is used to ascertaining the truth from the Bible themselves.

One important condition if we're going to see the discipling of our country, or indeed the world, in our generation, is that we get into a cycle of church multiplication like that of the rabbit churches. But it's possible that the elephant churches will have an important role to play in this: that the mature leaders produced by elephant churches can be a spiritual support to the rabbit church leaders. The movement might proceed at an explosive rate, but it takes time for people to mature. If elephant church leaders can recognise the promising and prophetic role of the rabbit churches, then they can play their role of encouraging the young rabbit-church leaders.

At the same time, the elephant churches can learn from the direct connection with God, from the passion for mission and from the flat fellowship structures of the rabbit churches and be rejuvenated themselves. I hope that both elephant churches and rabbit churches can play their part together in God's mission, carrying out different roles but working together in love.

Chain reaction mission

A chain reaction mission is basically when the gospel spreads across cultures through personal relationships. Because we live in an overlapping network of human relationships, these chain reactions can start up many times as the message that we have pass on to our family and friends spreads naturally, like a cold, to other networks.

But for the disciples to obey Jesus' command to "make disciples of all nations" (Matthew 28:19) and be witnesses "in Jerusalem, and in all Judea and Samaria, and to the farthest parts of the earth" (Acts 1:8), they needed to be strategically sent out to other cultures. That world mission is still not complete, as we still need people to sacrifice their safety and comfort and be sent out as workers to everywhere that God's beloved people live.

The account we have in Luke 10:1–3, where Jesus and the Twelve sent out "seventy two people," is a model of strategic mission where people spread the "virus of the Kingdom" to other areas in a chain reaction. Let's study the Upward, Outward and Inward dynamics of this story.

The essential part from an Upward perspective is to "ask the Lord of the harvest to send out workers into his harvest." (Luke 10:2) Since Jesus declares that the harvest is plentiful, if only workers went out into the harvest, they might meet people of peace. (see John 4:35) The problem is that there are not enough workers. If people go out into mission, sacrificing themselves for the sake of the Gospel, even as "lambs surrounded by wolves," (v. 3) this by itself would be progress for mission.

In this case, those "workers" would be those who were saved through the work of the seventy-two and discipled by them. The workers are themselves from the harvest fields, and sent from there into *other* communities.

The Lord commands us to pray for more workers to be raised up. The word that Jesus uses for "ask" has the meaning of a persistent pleading, like the widow pleading with the unjust judge. (See Luke 18) For about seven years ago now I have been praying almost every day with my prayer partner by telephone to ask God to raise up more workers for the harvest, and God has responded to those prayers and we have seen many workers raised up.

The essential part from an Outward perspective is the command to pluck up your courage and "Go!" For those sending people out, it may be worrying to send out those we have discipled into a difficult and dangerous mission field, and I'm sure many of those being sent did not want to leave the comfort of being surrounded by their friends and supporters. But we are expected to have confidence, to feel the heart of Jesus towards those who are waiting for the Gospel, and to move out with determination. The later we are at sending people out, the higher the risk of them depending on us—and us on them.

The esential part from an Inward perspective is that they are sent out in groups of two people who have the same aim. Jesus said that "where two or three are assembled in my name, I am there among them." (Matthew 18:20) If two people are in agreement with Jesus in their midst, they can efficiently deal with all of the various situations that come up on the mission field. On the other hand, a team of five or six have to take proportionally more time and effort, and usually end up handing everything over to a team leader. Two people loving and serving one another and working together in harmony is itself a powerful expression of the Kingdom of God.

As we pray for more workers in the harvest and send disciples out in groups of two, we can start a chain reaction mission that stretches even across cultural boundaries.

Knocking Over Dominos

13

Finding the person of peace

A university student came to Christ. When he was a child he had been in a traffic accident, and since then had been bound up by a fear of dying. Straight after he came to faith, he began to share with his friends and family about the existence of God, about God's love, and about the promise of eternal life. His testimony wasn't particularly well-polished, but out of all of the people who heard his story of meeting Christ, about one hundred people came to faith in a year.

This student was like the "person of peace" that Luke 10:6 talks about. You could say that the "person of peace" is the first domino to fall, someone who is at the center of the social network or community to which they belong. The important job for a worker coming in from outside is to touch that first domino to start the other dominos falling.

So how can we distinguish a person of peace? The person of peace will have three characteristics: they'll be like an OWL: O is for openness; W is for willingness; L is for leadership.

Upward, Outward, Inward

First, the person of peace will be open-hearted, showing concern for our work and being enthusiastic and willing to listen to teaching. But not all open people are people of peace. Those people with whom we come into contact with are not necessarily thirsty for truth. There are people who are just looking out for their own comfort and convenience. They do not want to apply the truth to their own lives and follow Jesus, and they are not willing to give up anything to gain eternal treasure; in other words, they want to use God in order to fulfill their own desires. "When trouble or persecution comes because of the word, immediately they fall away." (Matthew 13:20-21)

Second, the person of peace will be thirsty for the truth and willing to changing their life. But then, there are people who are thirsty for the truth but who are not concerned about the other people in their community. They are generally very busy with their own affairs and don't have enough in their hearts left over to have a good influence on their neighbours; their concern is self-centered, and they are more interested in self-fulfillment and solving their own problems than the spread of the Gospel or discipling or community building. They are people who "hear the word, but worldly cares and the seductiveness of wealth choke the word, so it produces nothing." (v. 22)

Thirdly, the person of peace is a leader who, at the urging of those outside their group, will shoulder the responsibility for mission inside the group. They perceive and appreciate the heart of God to make their friends and family into disciple-makers. They are the sort of person "who hears the word and understands. He bears fruit, yielding a hundred, sixty, or thirty times what was sown." (v. 23) The person of peace can activate the influence that they already possess within a community for the sake of the Gospel. The worker coming from outside the community has the responsibility of teaching the person of peace not just to make disciples, but to make disciples who make disciples. (See 2 Timothy 2:2)

It is the person of peace, and those around them, who are the real starting points of discipleship movements.

Is it the planter or the soil?

As you can see, the Bible talks about different kinds of soil which do not produce fruit. Do not be disappointed or feel supremely responsible if the person you thought was the person of peace suddenly goes away, or does not become outward-focused even though you've paid them a lot of attention. In many cases, the problem is not with the planter but with the soil.

Knowing this is a huge comfort to me. The average Christian life span for people in churches in Tokyo is three years; what I mean is that, after they get baptised, the average person stops coming to church after about three years. In the church I was part of, the rate of people coming in wasn't too bad but whenever someone stopped coming, I used to beat myself up about it. But look carefully at the parable of the sower. It doesn't say that the ground wasn't bearing fruit because the sower was sowing badly. In the parable, the skill or the nature of the sower wasn't considered a problem at all. What it was dealing with was the type of soil that the seed fell into.

It's difficult to understand the meaning of this parable if you're imagining a well-organised gardener who regularly plants nursery-grown seedlings into a well-irrigated field. But in the Middle East during Jesus's time, people would normally plant seeds *before* plowing a field, so people hearing this parable would clearly understand that the growth of the plant depended on the type of soil that the seed fell into, not on the skill of the sower.

Upward, Outward, Inward

I'm not defending myself, but seeing many people falling away really reminded me of that passage of Scripture again. Of course I recognise that there's room for the sower to develop their skills and giftings and become proficient, but the essential thing is to ensure that the seed sown in good soil grows well.

Out of the four types of soil, three did not bear fruit. But the encouraging thing is that in each community God has prepared some good soil, men and women of peace, for us. These are the people who will bear fruit, and the people who will open up future possibilities.

Cockroaches and moths

Out of the three types of soil which don't bear fruit, the seed which fell on the wayside got eaten by the birds and the seed on rocky ground was scorched by the sun, and both disappeared from sight. We can easily get discouraged and want to give up when we see these kinds of people going away from us. But the other kind of soil can be even more of a trap to us if we're not prepared for it.

The story tells how "other seeds fell among the thorns, and they grew up and choked them." (Matthew 13:7) In other words, the seeds aren't bearing fruit but they're still alive there under the thorns. This kind of people are always held back by "worldly cares and the seductiveness of wealth" (Matthew 13:22) and have no desire to follow the Word. Since they are not prepared to participate in the sufferings of Christ, even if they see that one problem they have has been solved, the next problem bubbles up and they just keep treading water.

But these people are not our enemies. God has brought the seed to their soil so that they may be saved. On the other hand, we do need to keep things in order of importance, as the number of workers is limited. Do not let other people spin you around with their problems, as you will end up burnt out and those who would "hear the word and understand" will be kept waiting.

Someone has compared the men and women of peace to "moths" and everyone else to "cockroaches.[1]" Cockroaches scuttle away from the light, whereas moths are attracted to it. If you focus on trying to catch moths instead of cockroaches, you can expect great things from God as entire familes, networks of friends, companies, schools and areas come to Christ. If you find the person of peace and help them to function as the person of peace, it's possible that between 30% and 100% of their whole group may fall into the Kingdom.

Approaching the person of peace

So how should we approach the person of peace? We'll explain it in Upward, Outward and Inward dynamics.

The Upward elements are blessing and prophecy. We are commanded "whenever you enter a house, first say, 'may peace be on this house!'" (Luke 10:5) If a person of peace is there, your peace will rest upon them. The passage also tells us that when we meet a person of peace, we are not to go from house to house but to stay in the house of peace.

When Jesus sent out his disciples, he didn't tell them exactly what to say, since they would "be given the message when [they] begin to speak." (Ephesians 6:19) We can assume that the disciples were to carry on the conversation prophetically as they were lead by the "Spirit of their Father." (See Matthew 10:20)

1   Neil Cole, *Organic Church: Growing Faith Where Life Happens*. San Francisco, CA: Jossey-Bass, 2005. p. 179

Upward, Outward, Inward

The Outward elements are service and evangelism. When Jewish people arrived in a town, the synagogue leaders would arrange for them to stay somewhere and they would be given food and lodging for two days. After the third day, the disciples would have to work around the house, serving the person of peace. One of the reasons that the disciples were forbidden from taking anything with them is so that they would have to do this and spend time with the person of peace. So as the disciples were working with and eating with the person of peace they would probably explain who had sent them to that town. They would testify that "the blind see, the lame walk, lepers are cleansed, the deaf hear, the dead are raised, and the poor have good news proclaimed to them" (Matthew 11:5) and they themselves would show God's power through healing the sick.

Finally, the Inward elements are repentance and fellowship. After Zacchaeus had invited Jesus into his house, he made this confession: "Look, Lord, half of my possessions I now give to the poor, and if I have cheated anyone of anything, I am paying back four times as much!" (Luke 19:8) In the same way, the person of peace would be convicted by the presence of God with the disciples and recognise that "the Kingdom of God has come" (Luke 10:9) and be prompted to change their lifestyle. Further, by being prepared to "eat what is set before you," (Luke 10:8) the disciples would express their humility and acceptance. Those who are coming from outside a community to share the Gospel must be careful that they do not take into that culture anything other than Christ himself.

Jesus declared that the harvest is plentiful. In other words, there are many people of peace all around us whom God has already prepared for us. God will use the person of peace to turn their community into a missionary people as those in the community are saved.

Knocking Over Dominos

Bless the "person of peace" who hears and understands the Gospel, prophesy to them, heal them, serve them, have close fellowship with them and lead them to repentance, and soon you'll be knocking over dominos...

14 Community Revolution

Planting a "church"?

Twenty years ago I wrote an article explaining that we needed to introduce small group dynamics into our churches, that the church would be rejuvenated as small groups share together the blessings and the troubles that people experienced in their day-to-day lives. But then ten years ago, I realised that it would be better to send out new small groups into the non-Christian world. Even if small group dynamics rejuvenated the churches, we would still be limited by the opportunities that non-Christians had to access these groups.

At that point I changed my mind, and thought that if people aren't going to come to the church, then the church needs to go out to the world. Passages in the Bible such as the commandment to fill the earth in Genesis, the story of the tower of Babel, Jesus's great commission and the Gentile mission after the persecution of Stephen all pointed not to a gathering but to a dispersing. If we go out into the world and witness, then people who don't really want to know about religious programmes can be attracted to the richness of Christ-centered fellowship and the Gospel can spread through human relationships. Small groups obeying the command to mission can testify to Jesus's love wherever they happen to be. The idea was that as a side-effect of this outwards vector, the groups themselves would be transformed internally.

But what I recently started to wonder is whether there's any need for us to start up our own, "man-made" small groups. The world is already full of small groups. If you go to any decent sized restaurant, you'll be able to literally see for yourself that people are gathered around tables in their own small groups and are already sharing life together. What the world needs is not more small groups but the presence of Christ himself.

When Jesus sent his mission team out in groups of two, they didn't go from house to house evangelising. They didn't pull one convert from this house and two converts from another group and put them together to start a Bible study. Instead they took the family relationships that already existed before they arrived and turned them into Christ-centered relationships. Jesus didn't tell us to go and plant churches, but to "go and make disciples of all nations," (Matthew 28:19) and a disciple is someone who has decided to love God and love their neighbor. What those disciples who went out two-by-two in Luke 10 brought was a new lifestyle of Honor God, Love Neighbor.

So when we say "make disciples," we simply mean having people live in an Honor God, Love Neighbor way: families and groups which meet together as community, following the values and boundaries of the Kingdom of God, and establishing relationships with other communities on the same principles. To put it in other words, transforming other communities into Christ-centered communities penetrated through with self-sacrificial love. God's plan is that the only true God will be worshipped in all kinds of cultural areas—politics, education, the media, the arts, leisure, religion, the family and business—and that God's rule would be evident as the whole community grows in righteousness, justice and love. (See Luke 4:18–19.) As we are guided deeper into community to love and support one another with the love of God, we can experience the realisation of Jesus's declaration that "The kingdom of God has come upon you!" (Luke 10:9)

Four steps to community revolution

Community revolution has four steps: preparation, declaration, education and evacuation[1]. Each two-person team who's trying to relate to a community from outside should go through each of these steps in three parts: Upward, Outward and Inward.

Preparation

As well as starting to knock over dominos, we build a close relationship either with the person of peace as they serve to support others, or with the members of the small group that the person of peace leads.

Upward   God shows us which is the appropriate small group to approach.

Outward   We start to relate to that small group. In cross-cultural mission, it may be necessary to have an extremely close working relationship with them. As we meet frequently and work together with the small group, we find out things like who the community's leader is, what the community's needs are, what sort of things would be necessary for that small group to be transformed, and whether the group has resources within it to be able to solve its own problems. When you're doing this, it is es-

---

1   David S. Lim, "Church @ the Frontiers: Transformation through Church Planting Movements and Community Development." *The Starfish Files*, Summer 2009. pp. 3–6. http://www.house-church.ca/resources2/107_Starfish_Files_Summer_2009.pdf

sential to have a good relationship with the community's leader.

Inward   The two-person team should serve as an example in the way that they live and in the way that they serve people through the fellowship of the small group.

Declaration

Once you have deepened relationships with the group through fellowship and through the way you live, you can start testifying through your words and through acts of kindness; at the same time, pray for the peace of the group that you are working with. You want to be creating a core group which brings discipleship and mutual support to the whole small group.

Upward   Pray for wisdom and God's guidance for friendship evangelism with the group leader and for forming a core group. Be aware of the authority that you have to bring about healing and miracles.

Outward   By listening carefully to the group leader and helping to fulfil their needs, praying for their peace, and through signs and wonders bring together a core group for community transformation. Start to disciple members of that core group as and when they come to faith. Discipleship goes hand in hand with helping them to support one another.

Inward   Become an example to that core group of how to share the Gospel and serve the community.

Education

This is where we help a core group to be able to independently support and disciple each other.

Upward   Receive direction from God about how that community can independently support itself.

Outward   With the consent of the community leader, and under the authority and suggestion of your core group, use the resources that are already in the community to develop a mutual support system.

Inward　　Encourage the members of the core group to love one another.

Evacuation

If a chain reaction of discipling begins to happen within the community, the two-man team can then leave the community, to allow independent, spontaneous gospel expansion to happen under the authority of the core group including the person of peace.

Upward　　Encourage the core group not to depend on the two-man team but to be directly connected to "God and His word" (Acts 20:32)

Outward　　The two-man team then leaves for their next outpost. If they leave too late, they can become a hindrance to the community's independence as the community begins to depend upon them.

Inward　　Tell the core group to "watch out for yourselves and for all the flock." (Acts 20:28) Since the two-man team has served the Lord and the group "with all humility and with tears" (Acts 20:19) their words will have authority.

An example from the Mizo people

Mission to the Mizo people of Mizoram in north-east India began in the 19th century. At the time they were a headhunting tribe but they experienced a community transformation and now they send out a huge number of missionaries. I think we can learn at least three things from this tribe.

The first point is to present the Gospel in a way that's appropriate to the mindset of the people you're evangelizing. The missionaries first tried to explain the Gospel in traditional concepts: God, sin, salvation. However, they soon noticed that the people had no sense of sin and so were not looking for a savior from sin. Their particular need was to be free from the fear of evil spirits that they believed lived in the forest. The missionaries started to talk about Jesus' victory over the devil and his power. As a result, they saw the phenomenon of entire tribes giving their lives to Jesus.

Jesus, similarly, didn't treat the man crying out for his sight to be restored to a lecture on doctrine. By understanding people's needs and fulfilling them, first, he led people to experience God's power, love and wisdom. Then he deepened his relationship with them, and only then did he address their deeper, spiritual needs: that was the order in which he dealt with people.

The second point is that they raised up local leaders. The Mizo are livestock farmers scattered over 80 different localities. From an early stage in their mission work, the missionaries were careful to train up local leaders in each area. They trained these leaders in fundamental doctrines and literacy skills, and on how to share the Gospel with their neighbors. Later, when the Indian government was worried that Mizoram was going to bid for independence, they threw out all the foreign missionaries to rid the area of foreign influence. But by 1989, there were 88 local missionaries to other local tribes supported by the Mizo people, and they have sent 50 missionaries to other parts of India.

These missionaries have no support from overseas but are supported by the people themselves. Every evening, the Mizo wives set aside one handful of rice for missionary support. The young men gather firewood and sell that, giving the proceeds to mission. They are not rich by any standards, but "their abundant joy and their extreme poverty have overflowed in the wealth of their generosity." (2 Corinthians 8:2)

The third point is that they have not merely done mission work but also community development, such as literacy and public hygiene movements. They have used the Mizo's own music to make mission songs, and the amazing stories of Mizo missionaries are handed down from generation to generation in local schools. The Mizo have taken responsibility, as a people group, for the spread of the Gospel, and they've made it their purpose in life. (See 1 Corinthians 9:18) Patrick Johnstone puts it this way: "No nation on earth has sent out a higher proportion of their people as missionaries than the Mizo[2]." Surely the day is coming when we will surpass their record!

A community can be transformed through a person of peace and a core group who take on the work of discipling and mutual support for themselves.

2   Rick Wood, "The Mizos of Northeast India: Proclaiming the Gospel to their neighbors near and far - Zari Malsawma" Mission Frontier, November-December, 1994. http://www.missionfrontiers.com/pdf/1994/1112/nd9412.htm (accessed April 09, 2010)

15 Leader Development and Coaching

Bananas and Banyan trees

In a certain town, there lived a famous preacher. His churches were full every Sunday and people surged in from near and from far to hear his masterful, living sermons.

But after he died, that same church closed down. There was nobody who could carry on his ministry. That man was such a gift from God that there were no workers who were even allowed to come near him while he was alive, and since nobody ever thought about who would continue the work after him, once he was gone, the ministry turned out to be a flash in the pan.

Paul Hiebert refers to two different plants, the banana and the banyan tree, to make his point about the importance of training 'leaders who train leaders.'[1] The banyan, popular in Japan as an ornamental tree, can grow up to 30 metres tall in its native India. Men and birds and animals can shelter in the shade under this kind of tree. But, as the proverb goes, "nothing grows under a banyan tree": no vegetation at all grows underneath the tree. After the tree

1   Paul G. Hiebert, "Banyan Trees and Banana Trees." In *Anthropological Reflections on Missiological Issues*, Grand Rapids, MI: Baker, 1994: pp. 173-175

dies, you can be left with a large empty space with nothing growing, sometimes up to an acre in size.

On the other hand, a banana is a very different kind of plant. Of course, it doesn't have the same impressive trunk and winding vines of a banyan, and it doesn't live for more than a year and a half, but it's just as powerful. Every six months it puts down a new bud, which grows into a fruit. All year around it blossoms and flowers, and the cycle continues until before your eyes it has grown into a banana forest.

Hiebert says that many leaders are like banyan trees. Banyan-style leaders have a tremendous ministry but have difficulty finding a successor, because they do not generate leaders, only followers. Followers are people who hang off their leaders' thoughts and follow their instructions. Since followers enjoy hearing their leaders' stories, the leaders can end up filled with pride. Leaders decide what the followers should learn and how they learn it, and the followers play their allotted role in the programme that the leader has drawn up. It's possible to grow followers in a relatively short space of time, and that's a useful result in its own way. But when the leader goes away, you are left only with a heavily dependent group of people, programmed with a list of instructions. This style of leadership strips away the potential fruit from an autonomous next-generation leader, and stunts the growth of the followers.

Growing leaders rather than followers is not a particularly rewarding job in terms of self-respect. If you're going to grow a leader, you can't just have them copy their teacher's thought and lifestyle—you need to encourage them to communicate directly with God, to think for themselves and to make decisions for themselves. But to do this is to entrust them with the ability to harbour doubts in their teacher's abilities and to raise objections to their teacher's proposals. If they do that, though, when they finally take over leadership for themselves, they can overcome the limitations of their predecessor, and carve out a new way for their new generation, based on the foundation of grace that they inherit.

So even if our young people are still 'diamonds in the rough,' even if they oversimplify everything, we don't need to nervously set about correcting them, but rather we must continue to encourage them to think things through on their own. More than that, we also have to encourage them, without relying on a textbook, to work out what are the issues that they need to grapple with and to take responsibility for, and we need to help them to focus their attention on those things.

This kind of teaching takes a lot of time and effort. As we dialogue together, as we give them opportunities to learn from their failure, we can develop them in a way that preserves and stresses their autonomy. But leaders who are developed in this way will be able to, many days later, discover their own giftings and take on responsibility for themselves, and the teachers will find themselves surrounded by young leaders who have surpassed them. For the teacher of leadership, this is a great reward.

Coaching

If we want to raise up a leader who makes autonomous judgements and works independently, we need to find a framework of development which is different from the normal model of mentoring where an older, more experienced person shares their wisdom, experience and knowhow with a younger person or new convert, mainly through encouraging words. 'Coaching' is the name given to the skill of developing leaders by standing alongside them as they receive guidance directly from God and actively put that into operation[2].

2   Mitsuo Fukuda, *Mentoring Like Barnabas*, Gloucester: Wide Margin, 2010

Upward, Outward, Inward

The coach takes an interest in what the young leader is saying, throws questions at them, encourages them and challenges them. Coaching is a personality-dialogue which assists the process of the personality-dialogue between the new leader and God.

Jesus was the best coach. The confession that 'you are the Christ, the son of the living God' (Matthew 16:16) is called the foundation of the Church, but Jesus didn't declare that on his own account; Peter confessed it himself. Jesus used a series of questions to help Peter to be taught directly by the Father.

In Upward Outward Inward training, we teach by using a questionnaire to coach our leaders. The questions are arranged into two sets of nine questions in a grid:

Personal	Past	Present	Future
Upward	What has God taught you from the Bible in the past week?	When do you particularly have a sense that God is with you?	In what ways will God deepen His relationship with you?
Outward	Who did you share the Gospel with, and how, in the past week?	Who amongst your non-Christian friends should you be serving, and how?	What can you practically do for the salvation of your friends and family?
Inward	Reflecting on the past week, is there anything that you need to repent of?	What are you currently wrestling with to help you become more Christ-like?	What choices will help you show love to the believers around you?

Team	Past	Present	Future
Upward	How have you helped others to come into an individual relationship with God?	Are your church members holding their devotions and accountability groups?	What is the next step to help your members joyfully follow God?
Outward	Please tell me about any people saved in your network within the past month.	How should people be training so that they can improve their relational skills?	What would be needed for you to start a new church?
Inward	What sort of things have hampered the unity of your mission team?	What can you do now to help others develop a passion for character formation?	What hopes does God hold for the relationships within your team?

The first set of nine questions cover issues to do with the trainee themselves, and the second set of questions deals with the mission team, church or movement that they lead. As the trainee answers each of the questions in turn, the plan is that, together with their coach and in the presence of God, they will be able to inspect themselves as to whether or not they are putting Honor God, Love Neighbor into practice in their lives[3].

Using the questionnaire

The aim of coaching is not fundamentally the growth of the client, but so that the growth of the client will impact upon the growth of the group or network they are leading. But just like a grandparent meeting their grandchildren, sometimes it's better to be involved in the growth of what we might call spiritual grandchildren or

3   Ken Takazawa, personal correspondence, 2007-07.

great-grandchildren. There are some things that you can help with as grandparents that parents can't do.

For children, the experience of being part of one big family, able to draw on a variety of resources, is an important opportunity to learn inter-generational communication and socialization. However, it's difficult to pass on the baton of discipleship beyond three generations unless you continue to keep focus on the growth of the mentee[4].

Let's now explain how this questionnaire works. The coach and the client agree to meet regularly for a coaching session. The sessions consist of four parts:

Prayer We start by praying to "God who causes the growth" (1 Corinthians 3:7) and ask for His protection and leading in the coaching session. Also we pray that we would be able to put into practice what we learn from God during the session, and that He would seal out any negative words or attitudes.

Review Looking back on the plan of action that was made at the previous coaching session, we review whether or not we could put that into practice. If we did, then we give thanks and celebrate God's goodness; if not, then we either look at the reasons and revise the aims, or we decide to continue wrestling with it.

Questions With both the coach and the client looking at the questionnaire, the client answers the questions in turn.

Decision We put together a measurable plan of what we want to achieve before the next coaching session, and pray together that we'll be able to achieve it. Then we look back over the session and talk over the most significant parts of it.

4   Takeshi Takazawa, *Coaching seminar for house church planters*. Unpublished handout from seminar held in Osaka, 2007-02-23.

Leader Development and Coaching

With the mentee learning directly from God and deliberately turning that into activity, the coach walking alongside him is able to raise up leaders and not just followers.

16 The Five Functions in the Church

What's your type?

There are some people who always have the same prayer request every time we pray together. For instance, one lady I know always says "please pray that I would be able to share the Gospel boldly!" This person always seems to enjoy evangelism.

Another young person says "I want you to pray that I'd get really close to God and then spend some really good time with my friends." When he sees a person who's hurting, he naturally comes alongside them.

In Ephesians 4:11, it says that Christ "gave some as apostles, some as prophets, some as evangelists, and some as pastors and teachers." I think we can say that the first lady is an evangelist, and the young man is a pastor. Sometimes I ask leaders the following question: "Let's say there are four people here. Who would you most like to spend time with? One is an emerging leader, one is a non-Christian, one is a person who's hurting, and one is someone who's a bit messed up in their thinking. If you don't particularly want to spend time with any of those four, that's OK as well."

I think that someone who chooses the first person, the emerging leader, could well have an apostolic passion, because the apostolic role is to grow foundational leaders for a movement and to share vision and strategy with them so that the can expand into a new area. Someone who chooses the non-Christian could be an evangelist. The evangelist is someone whose testimony and indeed their very existence directs the church outwards to the world, and who works out of a passion to see lost people meet with Jesus. I think someone who chooses the third person, the hurting person, may well have a pastoral gift. I don't mean that in the sense of a church clergyman, but perhaps we could say that they're someone who has a shepherd's spirit. The pastor knits people together and shows love to people who need care, so that they can grow and encourage each other in fellowship together and have a proper relationship with God.

Those who choose the fourth type of person, people with their thinking messed up, are probably teachers. They teach people who are confused and in error so that the church continues in the truth, and expound teaching from the example of the Bible. Not choosing any of them is the mark of the prophet. Many prophets are reluctant to spend time with people but like to spend their time with God; their role is to take what is on God's heart and share it with the church and the world.

Balancing the five functions

If one of these five functions begins to dominate, then the balance of the body is broken and it cannot grow or fulfill its calling. For instance, a church which is dominated by the apostolic function tends to leave things half-done as its leaders are always heading off in search of some new mission field and coming up with the next great idea before they've finished implementing the last great idea. A church full of prophets can, rather counter-intuitively, easily lose its way, because it can have a tendency to wait for God to intervene supernaturally and not properly value steady, concerted effort.

A church dominated by evangelists may see many people come to faith through events that are fascinating for non-Christians but not be up to the challenge of discipling them afterwards, and may end up merely repeating the same beginner-focused teaching. A church full of pastors sometimes flares up and then disappears. People gather in a church seeking healing for their hearts, and as they rush in all at once, the staff cannot keep up and end up burning out. A teacher-centric church depends on a pastor who always comes up with new information and moving insights.

Many of our churches are very dominated by the teacher function, whereas parachurch organizations are more likely to be dominated by evangelists. Sometimes we see our churches influenced by booming churches overseas which are strong in the pastoral or the prophetic functions, but churches with a strong apostolic emphasis are still pretty much unknown. The problem is that the people of God with their different abilities are each working in their own different way.

On the foundation of the apostles and prophets

What holds these five functions together is nothing less than the foundation of the apostles and prophets. (Ephesians 2:20) That is to say, apostolic vision and strategy for seeing the area filled with disciples of Christ, and prophetic listening to the voice of God for how to do that. The apostles read the map of where to send out disciples yet further away, and the prophets are like the satellite navigation system guiding people to that destination. The work advances within this framework as the Gospel is boldly proclaimed, as peoples' relationships with God and with each other are fixed up, and as we apply principles taken from the Bible.

Let's explain the foundation of the apostles and prophets using Paul's farewell sermon in Acts 20, looking at its Upward, Outward and Inward dimensions.

First, the Upward part is having a direct relationship with God. Paul does not hang on to the Ephesian elders but he entrusts them "to God and to the message of his grace." (Acts 20:32) Evangelists make people depend upon their programs, pastors make people depend upon their healing ministries, and teachers make people depend upon their insightful Bible interpretation; but the apostles and prophets are wanderers, and knowing that they will move on, want people to be taught directly by God. They want people to be able to carry on the movement without them after they leave. This direct connection to God means that when they hand the baton of discipleship onto the next generation of leaders, the doctrine and the spiritual quality of the work is not compromised; but if you keep on making a copy of a copy of what someone does, then you cannot expect to win a whole area or nation.

The Outward part is remembering the fact that the church is sent out into the world. The word "apostle" literally means "one who is sent." So John, who never went on an apostolic voyage, calls himself an "elder" rather than an "apostle." If someone is carrying out an apostolic ministry then they should be at the front line of mission. The prophet is sent out like the apostle (see Luke 11:39) to "encourage and strengthen the brothers." (Acts 15:32) The apostles and prophets show an example to the church by going out to the most dangerous posts, "compelled by the Spirit" (Acts 20:22) to remind the church of its identity as the missionary people of God.

The Inward part is that through the sufferings of the apostles and prophets, we see a servant-hearted lifestyle. Paul was used to "serving the Lord with all humility and with tears, and with the trials that happened to me because of the plots of the Jews." (Acts 20:19) They testify through their tears and through the humility with which they "follow in his steps." (1 Peter 2:21)

Building an apostolic team

People like the apostles and prophets who blaze a trail into new areas can't really be squeezed into a box, but you can find many innovative people who have the potential of becoming apostles or prophets, many of whom are non-Christians right now. They are outside the church, working as artists, musicians, business or social entrepreneurs, and authors.

People outside the church are really living out the message that the church should be sending out. There was an amazingly prophetic television programme shown on TBS late at night on the 25th of December 2009, called "2009 Christmas Promise." They got together a total of 34 musicians from 21 groups and sang a medley of their songs together. Each musician would sing their particular song, and then everyone would join in on the chorus. It was a medley lasting 22 minutes and 50 seconds, and there was such a feeling of unity about it. Musicians who are used to standing out from the crowd recognized each other, loved each other and respected each other, and showed their support for one another by singing a medley together. As I saw both singers and audience weeping, I thought, this is exactly what the church should be showing to the world.

Upward, Outward, Inward

Paul defined the church as "the body of Christ." The eyes can't do the job of the hands, and the head can't take on the work of the feet. (See 1 Corinthians 12:21) Each organ has to play the part that it is needed for, but they don't do that work alone. The body has many parts, but they are all knit together into one body. (See Romans 12:5) Unless we feel such as relationship that one person's joy becomes the whole body's joy, and one person's sadness becomes the whole body's sadness, then we cannot accomplish anything. Or rather, no matter what we accomplish, we will not experience God who is Trinity. In a fellowship that says "let me join in with your song," and in a relationship where we feel in our bones that "someone wants to sing my song with me," together the different parts can become one as we sing God's song together.

That doesn't mean that we always have to work directly together, but that we should respect each other, and that as a group we "fall in love with one another"; I think a group like that can start a discipling movement. "For it is time for judgment to begin, starting with the house of God." (1 Peter 4:17) When that time comes, the first thing that the church will have to repent of is its isolationism, that we have not worked together as the body of Christ. I think we'll be able to measure the progress of our movement as we see each area blessed with an apostolic team that is bound together like a family.

The foundation of the church is the apostles and prophets. The body of Christ has many parts, but God's mission will advance as we get the balance of our functions right, bound together in love.

A   Afterword

This book first appeared as a series of 16 articles called "Upward, Outward, Inward Training: Making disciples for Christ in Japan" in Revival Japan magazine from September 2009 to April 2010. The original title of the book was "Honor God, Love Neighbor," after a phrase used by Takamori Saigo, "the last true samurai." The phrase expresses the biblical lifestyle of loving God and loving your neighbor, and it's a watchword of the Upward Outward Inward way of training. The application of that Biblical principle to ordinary life has been the theme of the whole book.

By the way, I think that Takamori Saigo probably read the Bible and was influenced by it. In his collected teachings, he writes, "The Way is natural to heaven and earth. If a man is to follow it, he must make it his purpose to honour Heaven. Since Heaven loves me as much as my fellow man, I must love my fellow man as much as I love myself." Yoshimasa Moribe thinks that this "Heaven" refers to the God of the Bible.[1]

The theoretical basis of the design for this training can be found in my article "Experience rather than learning: examples of Japanese grass-roots discipleship."[2] This book

[1]   Yoshimasa Moribe, *Samurai who read the Bible*, Tokyo: Word of Life Press, 2009
[2]   Japanese Missiological Journal, No. 3, 2009, pp. 84-110

is the practical outworking of that theory, written as a reference work for those practically involved in grass-roots discipleship.

We need to prepare the infrastructure to allow a discipling movement to take root in the lives of ordinary Christians[3]. "Infrastructure" means the structures and facilities prepared as a foundation for business and for every day life, like roads, railroads, water and sanitation systems, telephone lines, harbors and communications media. For example, no matter how much you would like to use your mobile phone, if there isn't a base station near where you are, you won't get a signal. Those base stations and the lines they connect to are infrastructure.

The infrastructure for a discipling movement will be structures to help people disciple others in being connected to God, serving their neighbor, dying to self and living to disciple others; in other words, to help people live out Honor God, Love Neighbor. This short book is part of that infrastructure that testifies to the joy of being directly connected to Christ, and I hope it will be an encouragement to ordinary Christians. I pray that those who read it will begin to disciple those that they lead to Christ through their day-to-day lives. The network name is 'Jesus,' and the password is 'obedience.' So go on; access that infrastructure, raise up disciples for Christ, fill the earth with the glory of God, and let's bring revolution to the world!

---

3   Tony and Felicity Dale and the H2H team, "7% of American's attend a "religious service" at someone's home each week!" *House2house E-Letter*, January 14, 2010. `http://e-letter.house-2house.com/2010/01/14/7-of-american's-attend-a-"religious-service"-at-someone's-home-each-week/` (accessed April 09, 2010)

Afterword

About the Author

Mitsuo Fukuda is an equipper of disciple makers and founder of Rethinking Authentic Christianity Network, which has provided mission strategies and grass-root training systems for Body of Christ in Japan as well as in other Asian nations. After finishing the Graduate School of Theology at Kwansei Gakuin University, he researched Contextualization and Cultural Anthropology at Fuller Theological Seminary as a Fulbright Graduate Student and received a doctorate degree in Intercultural Studies. His previous books include "Mentoring Like Barnabas," "Paradigm Shift in Contextualization," and "Readings in Missiology: Japanese Culture and Christianity."

Breinigsville, PA USA
06 October 2010
246769BV00006B/2/P